Photography

G. S. Axelrod: 78 (top); courtesy of Jeffrey and Mary Frohock of Aquarius, Ltd., 2190 East Atlantic Blvd., Pompano Beach, FL 33062: 14, 15, 26, 27, 30, 31; bird trained by Shyne Browne, professional bird trainer for David Holzman of Sir Charles Bird Center of West Palm Beach, Florida: 155. Dr. H. R. Axelrod: 50, 54, 98, 122, 136. C. Bickford: 45, 154. Dr. A. E. Decoteau: 47, 67. K. Donnelly: 58. H.V. Lacey: title page, 16, 48, 124, 132. R. McMillan: 11. Dr. E. J. Mulawka: front and back endpapers, 6, 7, 10, 18, 19, 23, 130, 131, 134, 135, 138, 139, 142, 143, 146, 147, 150. V. Serbin: 22, 62. V. Serex: 57. Courtesy of Three Lions: 110. L. Van der Meid: 59, 70, 72, 73, 75, 78 (bottom), 79, 80, 88, 90, 97, 102, 109, 117, 118, 144, 145. Courtesy of Vogelpark Walsrode: 60, 151. World Wide Photo: 76 (bottom). E. Yamin: 25.

FRONT ENDPAPERS: Double Yellow Headed Amazon, *Amazona ochrocephala oratrix*.
BACK ENDPAPERS: Single Yellow Headed Amazon, *Amazona ochrocephala ochrocephala*.

Distributed in the U.S. by T.F.H. Publications, Inc., 211 West Sylvania Avenue, PO Box 427, Neptune, NJ 07753; in England by T.F.H. (Gt. Britain) Ltd., 13 Nutley Lane, Reigate, Surrey; in Canada to the pet trade by Rolf C. Hagen Ltd., 3225 Sartelon Street, Montreal 382, Quebec; in Canada to the book trade by H & L Pet Supplies, Inc., 27 Kingston Crescent, Kitchener, Ontario N28 2T6; in Southeast Asia by Y.W. Ong, 9 Lorong 36 Geylang, Singapore 14; in Australia and the South Pacific by Pet Imports Pty. Ltd., P.O. Box 149, Brookvale 2100, N.S.W. Australia; in South Africa by Valid Agencies, P.O. Box 51901, Randburg 2125 South Africa. Published by T.F.H. Publications, Inc., Ltd., the British Crown Colony of Hong Kong.

Yellow-Fronted Amazon Parrots

Dr. Edward J. Mulawka

Above and opposite: Specimens of *Amazona ochrocephala,* the Yellow Fronted, or Yellow Crowned, Amazon.

Dedication

To my daughter, Tamara Melony . . . May the joys of life fulfill the promise of her young womanhood.

E.J.M.

Contents

The author with a few of his pet parrots. The gray Cockatiel is called Tweedy Bird, the albino Cockatiel is Sylvester, and the Double Yellow Head is named Selsa.

Opposite, left to right: African Gray Parrot, *Psittacus erithacus erithacus,* Blue Fronted Amazon, *Amazona aestiva xanthopteryx,* and Double Yellow Headed Amazon, *Amazona ochrocephala oratrix.* Individuals of these three species are the best talking parrots.

Acknowledgments

No endeavor to write a book could be satisfied without the advice, knowledge and encouragement of friends and well-wishers. I am indebted to a great many people—far too many to mention individually—who have supported me in this endeavor. To all of them, my warmest thanks. I would especially like to express my gratitude to Dr. Thomas Howell of the Biology Department at the University of California (Los Angeles), who was particularly helpful in clarifying distribution problems of two of the subspecies of *Amazona ochrocephala* discussed in this book. Special thanks also go to Dr. Raymond Paynter at the Harvard Museum of Zoology, who searched through the museum's extensive files for data needed to clarify problems related to field expeditions.

Special thanks are also due to a variety of people who volunteered their time and birds so that photographs could be taken. Special thanks to Parrot World of Garden Grove, California and to its manager, Jack Golden, and his excellent staff for permitting me to have free access to whichever birds and facilities I needed for my photography. Thanks are also due to Theo Smelt of Garden Grove, California and Helga Nieberg of Costa Mesa, California for permitting me to photograph them and their birds. It was a pleasure to work with these fine people and their delightful pets.

I am appreciative also of the opportunity to photograph the excellent parrot stock at the Animal and Bird Pet Centre in Santa Ana, California. The Centre, owned by Dr. K. Svedeen of Mission Viejo, California, has more than once generously provided its facilities, staff and birds for my photography. I would also like to express my heartiest thanks to the owner and staff at Joy Bird Imports in Canoga Park, California. Their time and assistance were

12

generously given, and I cannot help but feel that I have acquired new friends as a result of the photo session there.

No acknowledgments could be complete without mentioning the Dave Schuelke family of Garden Grove, California and the Schuelke collection of exotic parrots. On more than one occasion the Schuelkes have graciously opened their household so that I could photograph their excellent collection. Their warmth, generosity and friendship are deeply appreciated.

Finally, I wish to acknowledge the influence that one of my pets, Selsa, had on this work. As a pet she was a delightful, cheerful and constant companion. Her presence in my household made life just that much more meaningful, and her antics were the original source of inspiration for the writing of this book.

Julio, a Yellow Naped Amazon, "falls dead" after being "shot" by Mary Frohock's finger.

Opposite:
Any bird that will lie on its back in its owner's hand is showing a lot of trust. Julio first started to "play dead" by falling over into his owner's hand (above). Julio also enjoys doing his "sexy bird" routine (below). He holds his tail up and says, "Look at the pretty bird."

Single Yellow Head, *Amazona o. ochrocephala,* fanning the feathers on its nape.

Introduction

There are approximately 8700 species of birds still inhabiting the world as we know it today. This number is of necessity inexact, for there is considerable disagreement among ornithologists and aviculturists alike concerning the status of various birds. Certain birds may be accorded status as full species by some taxonomists but given the rank of only subspecies or races by other taxonomists; there is a good degree of subjectivity involved. The Panama Amazon *(Amazona ochrocephala panamensis)* and the Yellow-Naped Amazon *(Amazona ochrocephala auropalliata)* are but two examples of birds about which there is widespread disagreement. Regardless of differences of opinion among taxonomists, however, the number of species still inhabiting the world is fewer than 10,000.

Of the approximately 8700 currently recognized species, there are only about 330 species that are considered parrots or parrot types. Unlike other families of birds, parrots are primarily restricted to semitropical and tropical regions. Specifically, they are common to equatorial regions. History tell us that various species have become extinct during the past five centuries. A good example of a common parrot type which became extinct during this century was the Carolina Parakeet *(Conuropsis carolinensis)*, which was the only parrot type common to North America north of the Rio Grande River. Even though its range was extensive (from Florida's Keys to the Great Lakes region) and it was a common enough bird in large numbers, the destruction of its habitat and the fact that it was considered a pest by farmers resulted in its extinction. The last known specimen died in a Cincinnati zoo in 1918. The Carolina Parakeet is not alone. Today numerous other species face a similar end.

Beautiful, easily tamed and able to talk—with such a reputation *Amazona ochrocephala* has a popularity unequalled among the Amazons. This delightful bird, named Skipper, is owned by Theo Smelt of Garden Grove, California. Skipper, seven years old, with an excellent disposition, has approximately eighty words in his vocabulary.

This parrot, called Oly, is just beginning to talk. He is a spirited and cheerful bird and shows a distinct preference for his mistress, Helga Nieberg of Costa Mesa, California.

Species extinction results from numerous causes, some of them more obvious than others. Many species are unadaptable and cannot maintain their numbers when their natural environment is dramatically changed, as occurs when forests are felled to make way for agriculture. Highly specialized and localized species such as island birds are particularly susceptible to habitat destruction. Such species have evolved in response to the specific characteristics of a given island and the opportunities that that particular environment may offer. Usually such species are isolated from similar birds on neighboring islands so that there is no exchange of populations. When the habitat is dramatically changed, when there is ruthless persecution to protect agriculture and when there is over-harvesting of the bird population, many of these species are unable to maintain their numbers and eventually fall into oblivion. The Cuban Macaw *Ara tricolor* is a good example of a highly specialized bird that was unable to adapt to rapid man-made environmental changes.

Critically speaking, however, while there is far less deliberate persecution of various species of parrots today because of the universal recognition of their economic value to the pet industry, the greatest present threat to parrots lies in the destruction of the few remaining rain forests circling the equatorial regions of the globe; over-harvesting also presents a problem. The Amazon region of South America provides an excellent example of what is taking place wherever parrot populations may be found throughout the globe.

The Amazon tropical rain forests have long been considered an inexhaustible and impenetrable region rich in life forms. Speciation is a constantly evolving force. It is currently estimated that there are over 10,000,000 different life forms inhabiting this region of the globe alone. And, by the most liberal of estimates, it is believed that fewer than 1,000,000 of these diverse life forms have been discovered, identified, studied and classified. Many of these life forms, particularly the vegetative forms, are critical in man's struggle against disease and old age. Yet the nations sharing the Amazonian jungles are felling the rain forests at an unprecedented rate in order to prepare more land for feeding their expanding populations. While scientists are scrambling to identify and study the diversity of life before the rain forests are forever gone, there is a foregone conclusion that because of the current rate of habitat destruction, the studies will never be completed.

Concerning parrots themselves, the destruction of this lush and natural habitat might not be quite the problem it is were it not for the fact that so little is known about most species of parrots. Indeed, unlike many other forms of avian and mammalian life with which man enriches his life, almost nothing is known about parrot behavior in either the wild or in captivity.

Given that many ornithologists and naturalists conducted extensive studies of the parrot avifauna over the past century and a half, it may seem incongruous to the reader that little is known of the behavior and life cycle of the various parrot species, particularly *Amazona ochrocephala*. Yet, in fact, this is the case.

The great ornithological studies of parrots and other avifauna in their natural environment took place primarily during the period between 1850 and 1920. It was a period of intense ornithological activity throughout the world. The scientific intent was to identify and classify all species of avifauna and their various races that inhabited the vast tracts of primitive forests still carpeting much of the globe. Each expedition was primarily a success, for in the countless sightings of diverse birds and the enormous number of specimens collected there were always new discoveries of either species or subspecies hitherto unknown to science.

Few ornithologists, however, ventured into the field to study a specific species, although on occasion such field studies were conducted. With the promise of so many species still awaiting discovery, few scientists could afford the luxury of specialized study.

Field expeditions therefore concerned themselves primarily with gathering as much data on as many species as possible. A two-month field expedition would therefore entail notations made on perhaps as many as several hundred species and races. Few notations would entail more than a line or two of comment.

As the great forests recede before the onslaught of man, however, conservationists, naturalists and ornithologists are frantically attempting to gather as much data as possible on all the species in order to establish refuges which will be conducive to the

One of the reasons so little is known about the behavior of most Amazons in the wild, especially the *Amazona ochrocephala* subspecies, becomes obvious in this picture of a captive *ochrocephala* in a pine tree. These parrots are able to blend so well with foliage that they often escape the notice of naturalists and ornithologists in the field.

Opposite:
A young Yellow Naped Amazon
A. o. auropalliata.

continued maintenance of stable populations of birds. In many instances, however, it may be already too late.

Amazona ochrocephala is only one of the twenty-eight currently recognized Amazon parrot species. While this species and its subspecies do not appear at this time to be faced with impending extinction, it is clear that in many areas where the birds were previously found their numbers have greatly diminished and in some localities they have been so over-harvested that sightings are considered rarities. The Panama Amazon *(Amazona ochrocephala panamensis)*, a perennial favorite among bird fanciers, is a good example of a parrot that is losing in the struggle for survival. While the subspecies is still common in some regions of Venezuela, the most recent studies of its distribution (during the 1940's and 1950's) demonstrate that it is found only in a very few localities in the Panamanian isthmus. Current studies would probably reveal that its territory has been reduced even more in the intervening period.

Even so, *Amazona ochrocephala* does not appear to be in imminent danger, but the continued harvesting of the species and the reduced natural habitat are making heavy inroads in populations. Additionally, some of the subspecies of *Amazona ochrocephala* occupy such limited terrains that only sound conservation measures can prevent over-harvesting and probable extinction. Additionally, where harvesting quotas have been established, smugglers have found illicit trade so lucrative that where sound conservation measures have been established they are easily circumvented.

While there is little that could be done to prevent the continued deforestation of habitat essential to species survival, an additional threat to survival results primarily from consumer demand for parrots as pets. The pet industry has found it more convenient to import wild stocks than to breed them in captivity, at least partly because of a lack of basic information needed if diverse parrot species are to be bred in captivity. That is not to suggest, however, that some commercial bird breeders and hobbyists are not breeding the various *Amazona ochrocephala* subspecies. In general, however, results are modest, and such successes are insufficient to meet consumer demands for the species.

A century and a half of ornithological study has provided little

A view of the Rio Aguaro in Brazil.

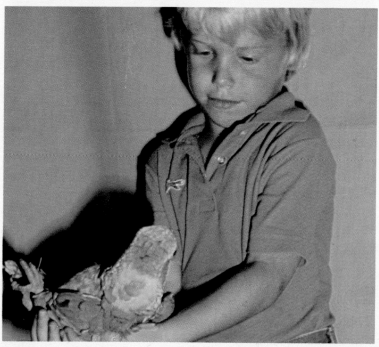

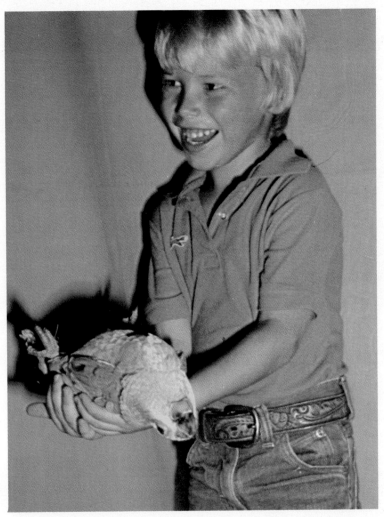

This is Julio playing "sexy bird" in Jeffrey Frohock's hands.

Opposite:
Above: Jeffrey and Julio having a discussion.
Julio can bark, crow, cluck, sound like a dive
bomber or like the ring of a telephone, ask questions and much more—all on command. Below:
Properly tamed and trained, this Yellow Nape is
easy for a child to handle.

insight into the life cycle and behavior of parrots, particularly *Amazona ochrocephala*. What ornithology provides us is scant at best.

Unfortunately, aviculture has not been very successful in breeding the birds in number. Aviculturists are saddled with a variety of problems inhibiting the development of a solid bank of data by which effective breeding programs can be established. Most aviculturists are hobbyists who are not scientifically trained in experimentation and data-gathering, and they are more inclined to breed those species of parrots which have already been bred in captivity. Further, *Amazona ochrocephala* does not reach sexual maturity until at least its sixth year, and even that estimate is basically an educated guess. They are expensive parrots to keep in captivity in the hope that there will be a return on the investment. And until recently there was no effective way of sexing males from females, so that the more adventurous and dedicated aviculturists frequently kept pairs for several years under conditions which were hoped would be conducive to a successful breeding—only to discover a number of years later that the "pair" were of the same sex. A truly frustrating and costly experience.

Finally, given the extreme scarcity of ornithological and avicultural data on the life cycle of the species, each aviculturist, whether hobby or commercially oriented, has been basically faced with beginning a breeding program without the benefits of scientific information. Each breeding program thus begun is basically a pioneering effort in which there is a great deal of failure experienced and only a smattering of success.

The various subspecies of *Amazona ochrocephala* are extremely popular because of their beauty, ability to talk and easy tamability, so it is a tragedy that more effective steps towards developing a scientific approach towards breeding this species have not been embarked upon to date. Because of their popularity as pets, and because demand exceeds supply, they are among the more expensive parrots.

The development of successful breeding programs would result in the development of a highly profitable industry. More importantly, it would do much to relieve the extreme pressure put on wild stocks of *Amazona ochrocephala*.

While this book is primarily directed at aviculturists in the belief that facts will result in insight, experimentation, innovation and eventually successful breeding programs, it is also intended to provide the amateur ornithologist and bird fancier alike with a basis of understanding the species's behavior both in the wild and under captive conditions.

Wherever possible, based on earlier published studies stretching over the past 150 years, details concerning the species's wild and captive behavior have been provided. Similarly, whatever published information exists on the mating, nesting, brooding and care of such birds has been included in this text. Finally, detailed physical descriptions of each race have been itemized so that the reader will be better able to distinguish one subspecies from the other.

It was initially intended that this book would contain photographs of nestlings, fledglings, young adults and sexually mature specimens so that the reader would be better able to identify each individual subspecies during the various stages of its growth and development. This objective was severely frustrated, however. With most subspecies, breedings are such uncommon occurrences in captivity that it was virtually impossible to locate among the thousands of breeders in the United States nestlings and fledglings of most of the subspecies. Additionally, at the time of the completion of this book, an embargo on the importation of exotic birds was in effect so that the usual stock of young and adult birds which arrive in quarantine normally during the early spring was not available for photography. Nevertheless, even with this extreme handicap, a serious effort has been made to provide the reader with such photographs as will be helpful in identifying the individual subspecies of *Amazona ochrocephala* and, where two subspecies are frequently confused, to provide photographs in such a way that readers can clearly see the distinguishing differences.

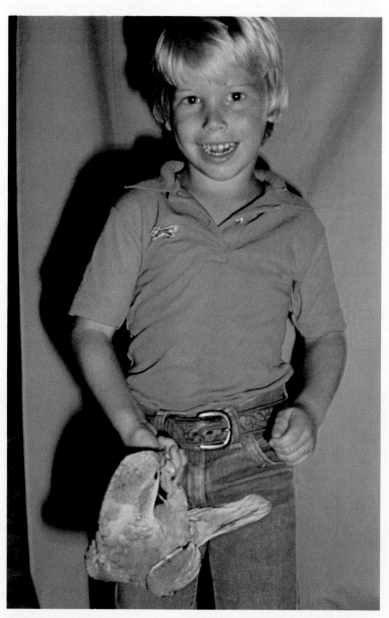

After being "shot" this time, Julio fell in the wrong direction.

Julio trying to show that he can do the trick (play dead) correctly.

Map of the geographic distribution of the five most widely distributed subspecies of *Amazona ochrocephala: oratrix* (cross-hatching), *auropalliata* (diagonal lines), *panamensis* (dotted areas), *ochrocephala* (horizontal lines) and *nattereri* (vertical lines).

General Characteristics
of *Amazona ochrocephala*

Under current classification systems, there are nine recognized subspecies of *Amazona ochrocephala*. There is some question concerning the true status of at least one subspecies (*A. o. xantholaema*) and the possibility exists that future research may result in a total reclassification of the subspecies into more than one species. At present, however, the different subspecies are:

A. o. ochrocephala
A. o. oratrix
A. o. auropalliata
A. o. parvipes
A. o. nattereri
A. o. tresmariae
A. o. belizensis
A. o. panamensis
A. o. xantholaema

PHYSICAL SIZE RANGE OF *A. OCHROCEPHALA*

The figures listed here are a composite of the sizes of all the nine distinct subspecies currently classified under the *A. ochrocephala* complex. There are considerable size differences between the various subspecies, so the figures listed should be considered only as a tool for defining the size range from smallest to largest.

	Wing	Tail	Culmen	Tarsus
Males	191-245mm	94-140mm	29-37mm	23-36.9mm
Females	190-233mm	92-136mm	29-36mm	23-34 mm

Females in each subspecies are generally smaller than males, but size alone cannot be used as a determining factor in sexing, because within any given subspecies some females are larger than some males. There are no visible sexual differences.

COMMON NAMES USED FOR THE DIFFERENT SUBSPECIES

A. o. ochrocephala: Colombian Amazon, Single Yellow-Head Amazon, Yellow Head Amazon, Yellow-Front Amazon.

A. o. oratrix: Mexican Double Yellow Head Amazon, Double Yellow Amazon.

A. o. tresmariae: Tres, Tres Maria Amazon, Tres Marie.

A. o. auropalliata: Yellow Naped Amazon, Yellow Nape Amazon, Nape.

A. o. belizensis: Double Yellow Amazon, Yellow Head Amazon.

A. o. parvipes: (Same as *A. o. auropalliata):* Yellow Nape, Nape, and Yellow Naped Amazon.

A. o. panamensis: Panama Amazon.

A. o. nattereri: Natterer's Amazon.

A. o. xantholaema: Since there are only two specimens known, this subspecies has not evolved a name through popular usage.

GENERAL COLOR CHARACTERISTICS OF ADULTS
Head Coloration

There are three basic color combination types common to *A. ochrocephala,* each type characterized by the distribution of yellow in a manner different from that of the others. The first type (*auropalliata, parvipes*) has a minimal amount of yellow on the forehead but an extensive amount of yellow on the nape; the second type (*ochrocephala, panamensis*) has the yellow confined solely to the forehead; the remaining group type (*belizensis, oratrix, tresmariae, nattereri, xantholaema*) has yellow over much or all of the head, including occiput, ear coverts, throat, hindneck and foreneck.

The amount of yellow on the head region or nape can vary from individual to individual, and the depth and brightness of the yellow can also have minor variances. However, the amount of yellow on the head region is always indicative of the group type to which the subspecies belongs. Usually, other characteristics as well will be useful in identifying the exact subspecies, particularly in the third group, which contains five separate subspecies that vary in only minor characteristics.

Table 1

	Wing	Tail	Culmen	Tarsus
A. o ochrocephala				
Males	200–222mm	106–125mm	31–36mm	25–27.5mm
Females	210–220mm	107–124mm	29–33mm	25–27mm
A. o. oratrix				
Males	217–245mm	108–136mm	31–37mm	24–27mm
Females	212–240mm	105–126.5mm	30–36mm	23–26mm
A. o. tresmariae				
Males	225–245mm	121–140mm	32–34.5mm	24–27mm
Females	226–237mm	130–136mm	30–32mm	24.5–26mm
A. o. auropalliata				
Males	215–234mm	106.5–125mm	34–37mm	25–29mm
Females	208–224mm	112.5–124mm	30.5–34.5mm	23–29mm
A. o. parvipes				
Males	210–240.5mm	107–127.5mm	30.9–34mm	31.7–36.9mm
Females	204–228.5mm	102–113mm	30.3–34mm	29.5–34mm
A. o. belizensis				
Males	211.5–220mm	116–120.5mm	31.2–33.5mm	33.3–35.6mm
Females *	202.5mm	106.5mm	31.5mm	32.9mm
A. o. panamensis				
Males	191–213mm	94–112mm	29–32mm	23–25mm
Females	190–212mm	92–109mm	28.5–33mm	23–26mm
A. o. xantholaema				
		no data available		
A. o. nattereri				
Males	218–238mm	119–126mm	31–35mm	26.5–28.5mm
Females	210–231mm	107–125mm	30–36mm	26–29mm

* Data based on measurement of one female specimen only.

Table of comparative dimensions of *Amazona ochrocephala* subspecies.

What green feathers there are on the head region not covered by yellow will vary between a yellow green, parrot green and blue-tinted green, according to the subspecies involved.

The beak is generally horn-colored in the northern subspecies but substantially more pigmented in grayish brown shades in the South American subspecies.

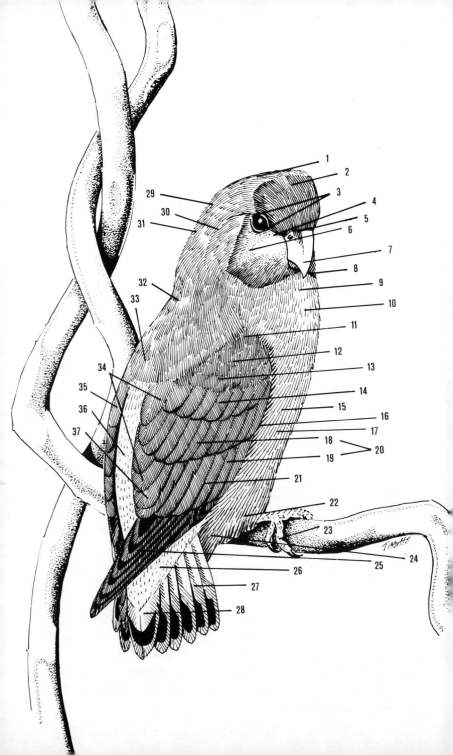

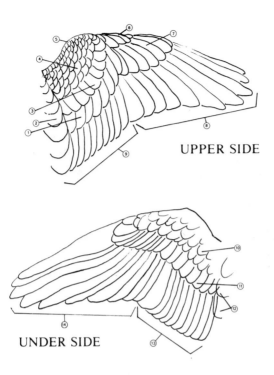

UPPER SIDE

UNDER SIDE

Wing
1. Secondary coverts. 2. Tertials. 3. Median wing coverts. 4. Lesser wing coverts. 5. Bend of wing. 6. Carpal edge. 7. Primary coverts. 8. Primaries. 9. Secondaries. 10. Lesser under wing coverts. 11. Greater under wing coverts. 12. Axillaries. 13. Secondaries. 14. Primaries.

Opposite:
Topography of a parrot (a Peach-faced Lovebird).
1. Crown. 2. Forecrown. 3. Periophthalmic ring. 4. Lores. 5. Cere. 6. Cheek. 7. Upper mandible. 8. Chin. 9. Throat. 10. Foreneck. 11. Bend of wing. 12. Upper wing. 13. Lesser wing coverts. 14. Median wing coverts. 15. Breast. 16. Carpal edge. 17. Abdomen. 18. Secondary coverts. 19. Primary coverts. 20. Greater wing coverts. 21. Secondaries. 22. Thigh (tibia). 23. Foot. 24. Under tail coverts. 25. Primaries. 26. Upper tail coverts. 27. Lateral tail feathers. 28. Central tail feathers. 29. Nape. 30. Ear coverts. 31. Hindneck. 32. Mantle. 33. Upper back. 34, 35, 37. Tertials. 36. Rump.

Wings

The bend of the wing is poppy red, but the amount of red is not extensive. In some cases it is unobservable if the wing is in a folded state. At times, there may be some yellow feathering at the bend mixed with the poppy red. Such yellow, however, is sparse. The carpal edge may be tinged in red or yellowish green.

The outer four secondaries are a poppy red with green or yellowish green basals. The primaries' basals are parrot green, gradually becoming a violet blue at the tips. Both over and under wing coverts are green, with the under coverts tending towards a definite yellowish green.

Body

The body color of the different subspecies varies from a yellowish green to dark parrot green on the breast and a dark parrot green on the back.

Tail

The tail is yellowish green to parrot green as per feathers on breast and back. The lateral feathers are basally red and there may be some outermost feathers tinged blue. Under tail coverts are yellowish green. Upper tail coverts darker.

Feet

Depending on subspecies, the feet range from a horny-flesh color to fleshy gray. The bottom thigh feathers may be tinged in yellow.

GENERAL COLOR CHARACTERISTICS OF IM-MATURES

Depending on race, there may be little or no yellow on the head area. There may be no red or yellow on the bend of the wing or carpal edge. The bill is gray. The iris is a chocolate brown. Until five or six months old, such immatures are often indistinguishable from the young of many other Amazon species.

GEOGRAPHICAL DISTRIBUTION

The nine subspecies of *A. ochrocephala* have a range extending from northern Mexico, stretching throughout Central America, and occupying most of northern and central South America. (For full particulars concerning the exact range of each subspecies, refer to the appropriate section of the chapter dealing with the individual races.)

BEHAVIOR IN THE WILD

A. ochrocephala, like almost every other parrot, is a gregarious bird. While solitary individuals are sighted from time to time, such sightings are generally exceptions. The bird is usually seen in pairs or small gatherings. At times, particularly during feeding or roosting, *A. ochrocephala* may be seen in groups numbering twenty or more individuals, with flocks of fifty (Monroe, 1968) not unusual. In some cases, however, the flocks may be considerably larger. In Venezuela, Cherrie (1916) observed flocks of the Single Yellow Head (*A. o. ochrocephala*) in groups of "two or three hundred birds together" during the breeding season, and Lowery and Dalquest (1951), while in southern Mexico, described the Double Yellow Head (*A. o. oratrix*) flocking behavior in the following terms:

> . . . on the coastal plain . . . literally hundreds of Yellow Headed Parrots were flying from their feeding grounds in the jungles of the humid division of the Lower Tropical Life-Zone, to their roosting grounds on the coastal plain. For an hour before dusk, from a few to a hundred parrots were in sight at all times, in pairs and small flocks, all flying to the eastward.

This gregariousness is common, regardless of race of *A. ochrocephala*. Almost every sighting of the species in the wild has stressed the fact that individuals are almost always paired with another, even out of the breeding season. Even when in motion in a flock, the members of each pair of individuals within the flock fly close together, with a marked distance separating one pair from another. An *Amazona ochrocephala* flock can be accurately defined as a congregation of loosely associated pairs of parrots.

In general, the species tends to prefer smaller gatherings of

Table 2

	Mexico	Belize	Guatemala	El Salvador	Honduras	Costa Rica	Nicaragua	Panama	Guyana	Venezuela	Colombia	Ecuador	Peru	Bolivia	Brazil
A. o. oratrix	X														
A. o. tresmariae	X														
A. o. auropalliata	X		X	X	X	X									
A. o. belizensis		X													
A. o. parvipes					X		X								
A. o. panamensis								X		X					
A. o. ochrocephala										X	X				X
A. o. xantholaema															X
A. o. nattereri												X	X	X	X

Table of distribution of *Amazona ochrocephala* subspecies in Central and South America.

several similar pairs (Friedman and Smith, 1950) except during breeding season, a time of the year when one would expect a more solitary paired behavior. At times there are exceptions. When Slud (1964) observed the Yellow Nape (*A. o. auropalliata*), he found the parrots to "occur singly, in two's and three's, and in larger groups ...". In the forests of the Tres Marias Islands, Nelson (1899) observed them flying in pairs, isolated from other pairs.

While the species prefer to pair, it is not certain whether such pairs are mated and, if so, whether such mated pairs remain together from breeding season to breeding season or whether the pairs are of identical sexes or pairs of opposite sexes which have no breeding interest in common. Since the sexes are alike in appearance, there is no way of assessing the relationship of a pair from a sighting.

Aviculture cannot supply the solution to the question of whether pairs remain mated over a number of years, as is true, for example, with various species of swans and geese. When a pair of *A. ochrocephala* breed in captivity, and over a period of time, does such a successful pairing represent a life-long interest in each other, or is it nothing more than an absence of potential partners to choose from? This problem could possibly be resolved by placing several individuals of the same species of both sexes in a large aviary, but most aviculturalists lack the financial resources and time to conduct such a long-term experiment, which may take several years to conclude before there may be an attempt by a pair to mate more than once, if they mate at all. Similarly, since *A. ochrocephala* is not readily bred in captivity, when a pair does show definite signs of interest in each other, other individuals within the flight are promptly removed lest they disrupt or nullify the reproductive interest of the pair.

Since most field expeditions collect specimens by shooting them and there are countless articles reporting the various subspecies thus collected, it could be safely assumed that pairs are felled in the collecting process. (The author recollects learning of one field expedition, whose details he has now forgotten, in which 13,000 birds were shot and skinned. There were numerous such expeditions.) Ornithological reports more frequently than not, however, fail to mention whether pairs were felled. As to whether such pairs are mated and would continue to remain as pairs over the years is highly speculative at this point.

While *A. ochrocephala* tends to fly in the evening to its roosting area en masse as a flock, the early morning flight behavior to the feeding grounds follows a somewhat different pattern. The pairs leave their roosting sites for the feeding grounds randomly, a pair or two at a time, until the roosting site is totally deserted. This process may take half an hour or more, depending on the number of pairs involved.

Food preferences of the various subspecies of *A. ochrocephala* are similar and probably vary only as a result of the minor differences that relate to the regional availability and variety of various fruits, seeds and other vegetation. Their main preference is for fruits, however, and the variety of fruits consumed will be limited only by geographic and seasonal factors. For example, Bailey (1906) observed *A. o. tresmariae* individuals feeding on figs on Cleofa Island, whereas Nelson (1899) found that the fleshy pods of *Pithecolobium dulce* were the staple part of the birds' diet. Howell's (1972) experience was that *A. o. auropalliata* preferred to feed in broad-leaved trees, no doubt an essential element to camouflaging themselves, a matter to be discussed shortly. The Double Yellow Head (*A. o. oratrix*) has been observed to prefer mangoes but, when banana plantations are in green fruit, will raid such plantations and cause considerable damage (Lowery and Dalquest, 1951). Similar to other observers in the field, Taylor (1860) reported that *A. ochrocephala* also feeds in cultivated maize fields.

Like numerous other species of parrots, *A. ochrocephala* is a creature of habit, preferring to feed in the same tree or at the same food source over a period of weeks. This habit, combined with the general tendency of the species towards tameness in the wild, has made it easy to approach during feeding. Nelson (1899) observed that even after hunters had stationed themselves under a tree waiting for the parrots to return in order to capture them, the parrots still continued to return to the familiar feeding place. As a matter of fact, in some cases they lack any semblance of wariness. As Nelson (1899) noted:

> A number of Yellow Headed parrots came down every
> day to feed in the trees, even among the houses, and did
> not pay the slightest attention to passing people.

Similarly, even when flocks have developed some wariness, or are faced with immediate danger, the species reflects a considerable tameness not found in other species. Wetmore (1939) describes such an incident:

> ... in low woods near the Rio Guarico many were
> feeding in the trees, seeming indifferent to my ap-
> proach unless I came quite near, and then flying for a
> short distance. Even when I shot one the others paid lit-
> tle attention though several saw the bird as it fell to the
> ground with a loud thud.

This general lack of wariness and appearance of tameness is in good measure related to the species remarkable coloration, which provides it with excellent camouflage while in the trees. Taylor's

(1860) description of their ability to camouflage themselves was well put when he noted that

> When they are in the tree tops it is difficult for anyone standing beneath to perceive them, as their plumage cannot be distinguished from the foliage.

This natural camouflage of the species has resulted in numerous anecdotal incidents. After a field expedition to study diverse birds in Mexico, Sutton (1951) recalled his first encounter with *A. o. oratrix*. After noticing a flock of eight individuals flying to a feeding site, he decided to stalk them. Standing beneath a tree, he was later to recount that

> All I heard was a low, steady, slightly breathing sound of munching, punctuated by sharp little clickings as pieces of pod hit leaves on their way to the ground.

Sutton recollected that he had stood under the tree for some time without sight of the parrots, and during this entire period the debris from the feeding continued to rain all about him. Finally,

> a big, dry, neatly chambered pod, tough as a piece of coconut shell and astonishingly heavy, dropped straight on my head. Had not an old Mexican proverb warned us that he who sneaks under breakfast tables may well expect a crumb in the eye or a kick in the face?

When feeding, aside from the kinds of feeding sounds mentioned by Sutton, the species is quiet and so secure in its camouflage that it is difficult to flush the parrots from their feeding activities. Forshaw (1977) observed that when he was able to flush the parrots

> ... these parrots fly out from the opposite side of the crown, and although there is an audible flapping of wings as they leave, there is no screeching until they are well away from the tree.

Just as it pairs in flight and in roosting, *A. ochrocephala* prefers to feed in pairs (Stager, 1957). When the "parrots have finished their feeding at about half past ten o'clock, and departed two by two, each of the four pairs keeping close together in flight, their wings beating rapidly, ibis fashion, as they sought cool retreat in lower parts of the trees, " (Sutton, 1951) they normally spend the remainder of the day between feeding periods generally paired while resting in the midday heat. This time of the day is generally spent in snoozing, mutual preening, low-keyed clucking and similar satisfaction noises. There are usually one or two pairs to a tree. While Sutton observed that *A. ochrocephala* preferred the lower branches of the trees during the non-feeding midday rest period, the general tendency of the species is to choose the tallest trees available during these inactive periods. Miller's (1947) account, for example, is representative of most of the observations made:

> A favored kind of tree was one which rose to heights of one hundred feet or more and bore conspicuous, large orange flowers. The amazons moved from crown to crown characteristically in twos. . .

The type of tree chosen during these non-feeding and non-roosting periods is no doubt related to a variety of factors, the most outstanding being perhaps the presence of danger, the heat of that particular day and the availability of towering trees, particularly in forests bordering savanna terrain and agricultural areas. Most observations, however, strongly suggest that whenever possible *A. ochrocephala* will choose the most towering trees.

When startled, the species may or may not cry out. Slud (1964) found that when startled the Yellow Nape (*A. o. auropalliata*) generally took off ". . . silently, excepting for flapping sounds . . .", while other observers have found the exact opposite to be true; as Sutton (1951) noted, they departed by "squawking like demons."

Towards late afternoon and evening they can be seen flying in pairs towards their roosting places. Usually, since *A. ochrocephala* appears to be a parrot of habit, it tends to favor the continued use of a favored roosting area.

As each pair departs for the roosting place, its usual flight is at a considerable altitude. As a matter of fact, in discussing the escaped *A. ochrocephala* in the Los Angeles area, for example, Hardy (1973) concluded that "it is clear that these birds are wide ranging, merely from observations, individuals flying at great heights completely out of sight of an observer." During the flight to the roosting areas the flock reassembles as pairs arrive in a continuous

A. ochrocephala in the wild.

flow. During these flights, regardless of when they occur, their flying behavior is similar to that of a duck in its rate of beat and steadiness (Miller, 1947), most of the downstroke of the wings ending well below the body.

As they fly towards their roosting place their flight is often accompanied by screaming and chattering (Taylor, 1860). Miller (1947) has likened this squawking to that of a "group of crows." Other observers have described their cries as an ' *ork, ork, ork* ' and *"carrow, car-r-r-row"* (Sutton, 1951) or *"cacawuk"* (Friedman and Smith, 1950). Slud (1964) feels that the Yellow Nape's (*A. o. auropalliata*) cries are ". . . very human sounding calls that bring to mind a person trying to imitate a parrot. More frequently than not, the species has a disagreeable and harsh sounding call, particularly when it is distressed.

A. ochrocephala proves itself a remarkably adaptable creature. While it prefers wooded regions, usually showing a preference for the drier woods (although in various localities it has shown a preference for the more humid forests), it is equally at home in the savannas and cultivated areas. Some reports find the species to prefer towering trees, such as in the tropical regions of Colombia (Miller, 1947) and in other instances trees and shrubbery no more than fifteen to thirty-five feet high. The size of acceptable and preferred tree height seems to be more of a "what's available" choice than "all or nothing."

Their adaptability no doubt accounts for their ability to apparently maintain their numbers in the wilds despite relentless and ruthless harvesting. *Amazona ochrocephala* appears to display the same type of adaptability common to crows and ravens, which persist in maintaining their numbers, indeed even increasing them in extensively developed agricultural areas, even though they are ruthlessly shot for the damage they cause to crops.

Perhaps the species' capacity to adapt might well be illustrated by the accounts of observers who have studied specimens that have escaped into environments totally alien to those they have enjoyed in their own native lands. In some cases, the species shows not only an exceptional ability to adapt but also an outstanding hardiness.

It is not uncommon for pet parrots to escape captivity and revert

Amazon parrots in flight.

to their former wild habits. Some question about their survival capacity in a geographical area such as Los Angeles can be raised, particularly in view of the facts that the Los Angeles temperature during the winter can drop substantially and that the available food supplies are significantly different from those of more tropical regions. Yet *A. ochrocephala* seems to have no difficulty surviving as an escapee in the Los Angeles area. As Hardy (1973) points out, several flocks numbering between four and thirty have been observed; these flocks have not only been able to maintain their numbers, in some instances for an estimated ten years, but their continued presence in the same areas illustrates their adaptability and hardiness. Hardy notes that not only have the parrots adopted a special fondness for tangerines and walnuts growing in neighborhood backyards but also that they have become so selective in their food preferences that they will waste the flesh of oranges just for the seeds inside. While Hardy's findings may not be entirely surprising for most students of ornithology, of greater ornithological interest is John Bull's (1973) article on escaped exotic birds in New York City in which he says, "A few have

Monk Parakeets, *Myiopsitta monachus*, are another example of parrots escaping captivity and establishing wild populations in a geographic area totally unlike their native environment. It is presumed that the Monk Parakeets found wild in the New York region escaped from a shipment at Kennedy Airport sometime during the 1960's. Attempts have been made to control these parakeets (by destroying their nests) because the birds are pests of grain fields and fruit crops.

escaped and two even survived the northern winter by feeding on crabapples."

While it was common practice in Europe, particularly England, during the last century, and still is to a modest degree among some aviculturists and bird fanciers, to allow their *A. ochrocephala* full freedom or partial freedom the entire year with the expectation that the birds would survive the winter, the survival of the Yellow Fronts and other parrots is really not too amazing when one considers that enclosed shelters were provided for the birds so that they could 'home in' when the weather was inclement. But the New York *A. ochrocephala* had no such sanctuary which could provide them with food and shelter from the winter's cold.

Additionally, aside from the threat of starvation and cold with which the birds had to cope, the danger from men must certainly have been of at least equal significance. Green birds with yellow heads are not the kind of wild avifauna one normally observes in New York City. The threat from B.B.'s, stones and various other types of missiles must have been considerable.

The fact that the species is able to adapt, given such threats, particularly those from men, suggests that the species develops adaptive behaviors to meet with dangerous circumstances. I have, for example, on two occasions seen *Amazona ochrocephala* in small flocks in the Balboa Island-Newport Beach region of southern California, a heavily populated area. In both instances—one a flock of four and the other a flock of six—Yellow Fronts flew high overhead in the evening. The flight was always well above the highest trees. A librarian at the Los Angeles County Museum, adjacent to the University of Southern California in downtown Los Angeles, informed me that a large flock of fifteen to twenty Amazons has survived for several years in that locality. A fellow librarian who is familiar with some parrot species noted that the flock was comprised primarily of *A. ochrocephala*. Several of the Museum's employees have observed the flock on a variety of occasions, but the parrots are usually seen only in the twilight hours.

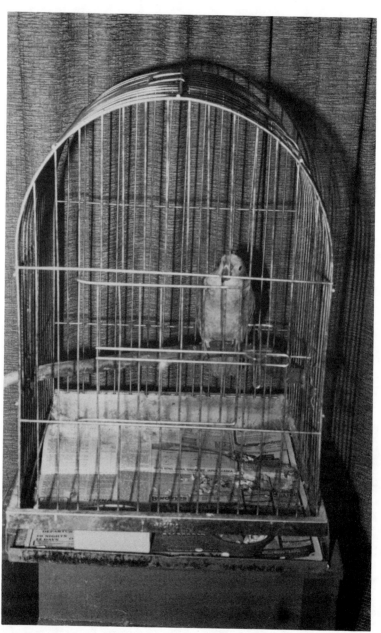

Cages for Amazon parrots should be large enough that the bird can fully stretch its wings. This particular cage has a tray which pulls out to facilitate cleaning.

A. ochrocephala in Captivity

The Yellow Fronted Amazon in its various subspecies has long been considered a highly desirable pet because of its striking ability to mimic what it hears, its colorful plumage, easy accessibility and delightful personality. The species has an international reputation, with credentials which rank it among the most talented of all parrot species. While there are numerous other parrot species which will produce individuals which may talk or have colorful personalities, *Amazona ochrocephala* consistently produces individuals which surpass all others, except perhaps for the Blue Fronted Amazon, *Amazona aestiva*, or the African Grey, *Psittacus erithacus*.

No doubt the Yellow Fronted's popularity stems considerably from some of the earliest observations of the species in the wild, where (as was discussed earlier) it was readily observed that the species appeared quite tame. Grayson (1871) had earlier reported briefly on the bird's tameness and the ease with which it could be captured during 1865, and thirty years later Nelson (1899) had found that despite heavy harvesting the species was still tame enough to be captured easily. He described the manner in which they were captured as follows:

> By means of a noose on the end of a long cane, like a fishing rod, many old parrots are captured while feeding. An old woman had twenty birds which she had taken in this manner while they were feeding at the top of a small *Pithecolobium* tree by her door. The hunters search for regular feeding places in the forest and wait under trees for the birds to come. When the birds arrive, the end of the rod is slowly and cautiously pushed

51

up through the branches, the noose slipped over the bird's head and drawn about its neck with a quick jerk, after which the victim is hauled down and thrust into a cage.

No doubt such methods of capture were probably utilized wherever the species habituated feeding grounds where the trees were not excessively tall.

While adult specimens were easily capturable, it was the young—just as today—which were more desirable as pets and for which considerable effort was often expended to locate and capture them. The capture of the young, while not requiring as much cunning, nevertheless entailed a considerable amount of expertise so that an appropriately aged chick would be taken from the nest. Nelson (1899) continues by noting:

As these birds readily learn to talk, they are highly prized as pets, and are sold to visitors, or sent to towns on the mainland; the birds taken while young being most highly prized on account of their docility. The men search for their nests, and when one is located the hunter strikes the base of the tree several sharp blows with a stone or ax, and then places his ear against the trunk and listens. He can tell whether the young are old enough to remove by the strength of the cries in response to the blows on the tree. Being satisfied of the presence of his game, the hunter climbs the tree, and if necessary cuts into the nest with his machete. Each brood contains two young, which are carried to the ground inside the hunter's shirt.

Young birds have long been preferred to older birds, a preference strongly related to the over-all personality dispositions of most *A. ochrocephala* subspecies. With the possible exceptions of the Panama Amazon (*A.o. panamensis*) and Yellow Nape Amazon (*A.o. auropalliata*), most Yellow Fronted Amazon subspecies have a reputation for being unpredictable if attempts to tame and train them are undertaken when they are already mature. While Yellow Fronted Amazons have a colorful personality as compared to other members of the genus, their colorfulness and mischievousness are closely associated with their tendency towards excitability.

52

Since individual personalities differ from one bird to another, there is no way of predicting the outcome of the taming process on an adult Yellow Fronted Amazon, and there is no way of determining beforehand whether a given wild adult Yellow Front will develop the kind of talking ability for which the species is noted. Indeed, while most Yellow Fronts can be delightful and affectionate pets, and while the majority can learn to mimic well, the Yellow Front which both mimics and is also an affectionate pet is the exception rather than the rule.

Their behavior more often than not is highly unpredictable in the sense that it is difficult to predict from day to day the species' general disposition. A great many individuals reveal unique individuality, a tendency to become extremely excited and volatile at times and a considerable amount of intelligence and imagination. But the qualities that make this species highly desirable are often the same qualities that can be detrimental. Mature Yellow Fronts with rigid personalities have a tendency to bite at the merest provocation, will reject any bond between master and bird, may display some affection one day and then bite the object of their affection the following day without provocation, and so on.

Nevertheless, despite the element of unpredictability common to many individuals, *A. ochrocephala* has always been held in high esteem. As a matter of historical interest, the Yellow Fronted Amazons were so popular in Great Britain during the last century that it was a common practice for wealthier estate owners to release them in the woods on their estates, often in considerable numbers. These flamboyant exercises in attempting to create a semblance of a tropical environment in a somewhat damp and cold England were in large part encouraged by the species' hardiness although in fact numerous other, more delicate species were also expected to endure Britain's climate. The Yellow Fronts were expected to forage during the day and return to their cages in the evening. While there may have been a relatively high mortality rate caused by Britain's generally inclement weather, the late nineteenth century aviculturist Dr. W.T. Greene (1884) lamented that the greatest problem faced by the Yellow Fronted Amazons was the hunters, who took a heavy toll whenever new Yellow Fronts were released.

Yellow Naped Amazon, *A. o. auropalliata,* being trained to step from hand to hand.

There has long been a conflict arising from the species' general unpredictability on the one hand and its continued popularity as one of the most prized of the Psittacidae on the other. The conflict for the most part has been rationalized and thereby resolved by emphasizing the desirability of immature individuals in preference to mature birds. In his discussion on *A. ochrocephala,* Dr. Greene wrote:

> Such parrots . . . rarely become tame and never make good talkers [i.e. captured matured birds]; to educate thoroughly one of these creatures it must be brought up from the nest by hand, and by the time it can eat alone . . . (it will) . . . probably have learned to repeat some words, if not a sentence or two.

While British ornithology during the nineteenth century made significant and outstanding contributions to the scientific study of birds throughout the world, British aviculture was notorious for its lack of even the most basic of essential practices needed to maintain parrots and other exotic birds, a matter which Greene himself lamented about on several occasions in his writings. As he also frequently observed, exotic birds rarely survived long in captivity while in Britain, a misfortune not as frequently experienced by Continental aviculturists in Europe. Dr. Greene, nevertheless, attempted to make a case for the proper care of parrots by insisting that, contrary to British avicultural practice during that day—a practice considered abominable by Continental European aviculturists—*parrots should indeed by given sufficient drinking water each day, for seeds alone did not provide sufficient moisture!* (His concern, incidentally, often seemed to focus more on the bird's agony for lack of water than on its need for water for survival!) Lack of water would not present itself as a problem except that birds received only dry seeds for food. Similarly, it was common fashion for the British to hand-feed chicks with bread soaked in milk. Given Britain's notorious mortality rates of exotic birds during the period involved, it would be interesting to speculate about how Greene would propose to keep young *A. ochrocephala* alive long enough to enjoy their newly acquired vocabularies and tameness.

Given contemporary understanding of parrot care and nutritional needs, Greene's dilemmas are somewhat comical, if not tragic, because of the kinds of losses which must have been suffered by British bird fanciers and aviculturists. It may be of interest for the reader to know that while many infant *A. ochrocephala* chicks are taken from their nests each year in Central American and South American countries, few captive infants are lost. On several occasions, while in Mexico, the author has seen surrogate human mothers mash maize and various cereals in their mouths and then proceed to feed the chick by allowing the youngster to stick its head into the mouth and eat the mashed contents much in the manner the chick would eat if fed by a parent regurgitating its food. This practice, incidentally, is common in many regions of the world.

Sometimes there is such a demand for young chicks that the consequences can often be comical. On several occasions, while travelling in Mexico, particularly in the border regions near the United States, I have seen numerous *A. ochrocephala* chicks being offered for sale, primarily to the tourist trade. Usually, these fledgling Yellow Heads are a fraction of the cost one would normally expect to pay in the U.S.

Because of the considerable savings involved, many U.S. tourists are willing to risk being caught smuggling such youngsters across the border. When sales are brisk and demand for fledgling Yellow Heads exceeds supply, some enterprising Mexican entrepreneurs are quick to seize upon the tourists' greed and naivete. On several occasions the author has had the opportunity of seeing the young of other parrot species such as the Green Cheeked Amazon (*Amazona viridigenalis*) with their heads dyed a brilliant yellow from forehead to nape. These unfortunate victims, I am told, are simply dunked into a vat of yellow dye after which their beaks are cleaned. Since the young of most Amazons are primarily green, it is often difficult to distinguish one *Amazona* species youngster from another.

On one occasion, I received a telephone call from a total stranger who expressed considerable concern about five of his "Mexican Double Yellow Heads"—it seemed that the youngsters were turning green on their heads, and he wondered if that was 'normal' in the maturing process. When the fledglings were brought to me for my inspection and opinion, it was obvious that the caller, apparently an accomplished and seasoned smuggler, had allowed his greed to better his judgment. I discreetly inquired about their origin.

"Oh, they're home raised," was the reply. When I pointed out to him that the five birds in question had the finest and most brilliant yellow I had ever seen for a Green Cheek, he confessed sheepishly that he still had another six at home.

While there is a persistent demand for the young of *A. ochrocephala*, mature birds provide by far the majority of parrots offered for sale to the public, particularly after the nesting season has finished and chicks are no longer available.

There is no question, however, that whether young or old *A. ochrocephala* is an excellent talking parrot, perhaps the outstanding talker in the parrot world. Many writers have extolled the speaking ability common to the species. The Reverend F.G. Dutton (Greene, 1884), a contemporary of Dr. Greene's, himself an aviculturist and ornithologist of sorts, when speaking about one which he had purchased for a pet, typifies the attitude of the countless owners of the species who swear by its excellence:

Two seven-week-old Double Yellow Heads, *A. o. oratrix*. The black nails and tongues of these young birds will become flesh-colored at about twelve weeks of age, and the area of yellow on the head will become more extensive after about eight months of age.

> It [*A. ochrocephala*, subspecies not mentioned] sang several songs, did the soldier's exercises, and many other phrases all of which it repeated whenever I wished it.

It might be interesting to note that the Reverend Dutton had acquired the parrot in Brest, France from a Frenchman who had been a lifelong sailor. According to the account, the parrot was not only an accomplished and competent talker but also had acquired a profuse vocabulary of French vulgarities and obscenities, so the good reverend was finally obliged to sell the bird.

While *A. ochrocephala* enjoys a well established international reputation for talking, there is considerable debate as to which subspecies are better talkers than others. General opinion favors the Yellow Nape (*A. o. auropalliata*), Panama (*A. o. panamensis*), Double Yellow Head (*A. o. oratrix*) and Tres Marias (*A. o. tresmariae*), with the remainder of the subspecies lumped together as more or less indistinguishable. Whether or not this hierarchy is an accurate assessment is debatable, for there is no concrete evidence one way or another. Indeed, the varied views offered by numerous observers suggest contradictory opinions; more often than not, tradition and local chauvinism color the final assessment made about any given subspecies. This dilemma is identical to the heated debates which occur over whether *A. ochrocephala* or *Psittacus erithacus* is a better talker. Since Europeans have almost two thousand years of involvement with the African Grey, and because that bird is more easily obtainable by Europeans, the consensus in Europe is that *P. erithacus* is better without a doubt; North Americans, however, have easier access to the varied *A. ochrocephala* subspecies and therefore are inclined to argue that that species is superior.

As noted above, opinions are varied. Herklots (1961) observed that Trinidadians believed that their *A. o. ochrocephala* was

Different styles of parrot cages.

A tame Yellow Nape, *A. o. auropalliata,* on the left and a tame Double Yellow Head, *A. o. oratrix,* on the right. Both of these *ochrocephala* subspecies are considered to have superior talking abilities.

superior to other subspecies. Nelson (1899), in his studies on Las Tres Marias Islands, noted that the islanders viewed their bird as an unexcelled talker. Slud (1964) noted about the Yellow Nape that "its reputation as one of the best talking parrots is deserved." Cherrie (1916) found that *A. o. ochrocephala* was more highly prized than all other subspecies in the Venezuelan Orinoco region. Basically, regardless of the wide variety of parrots and parrot types available to the residents of any given tropical region, whatever subspecies of *Amazona ochrocephala* is common to that region will be considered the best of all the parrot species found in that region.

In the non-tropical regions, opinion will not be so much shaped by local chauvinism as by a variety of factors, generally the most important factor being exposure to a given race of *A. ochrocephala.* For example, as noted earlier, the general consensus is that the Yellow Nape and Panama are the two best talkers, while the Double Yellow Head and Tres Marias are third and fourth (not necessarily in that order) among the recognized subspecies of *A. ochrocephala.* Plath and Davis (1971), whose book *This is the Parrot* is a common reference text in many homes, describe the Mex-

Panama Amazon, *A. o. panamensis,* one of the best talking parrots. Additionally, the Panama is easily tamed and proves to be an affectionate pet.

ican Double Yellow Head as trainable "to become an excellent talker and singer" and the Yellow Nape as being a ". . . close rival to the Yellow-Headed Amazon in talking ability." The same authors, however, totally ignore the talking ability of the Panama and Tres Marias.

Similarly, Bates and Busenbark (1978), two extremely knowledgeable aviculturists and authors of several books on parrots and related birds, are quite definite in their opinion when they state about the Yellow Nape that "if there is another species of parrot that is as consistently a good talker . . . the writers have never come across it" and that *A. o. auropalliata* is an excellent candidate for the development of an extensive vocabulary. But then a few pages later, the same authors describe the Panama *(A. o. panamensis)* as "an unexcelled talker."

Lest it be construed that Plath, Davis, Bates and Busenbark or this present writer are confused and contradictory, let the reader be assured that such a conclusion is far from the truth. The fact is that there are so many outstanding talkers among the four races briefly discussed above, and indeed among all the others within the *Amazona ochrocephala* complex, that as soon as one is forced to make a judgment as to which subspecies is best, one or several individuals from one of the other *A. ochrocephala* subspecies immediately come to mind and seem superior.

My personal opinion is that the Yellow Nape is best, followed by the Panama, the Double Yellow, Tres Marias and Single Yellow. The reader, of course, is left to his own judgment as to whether or not these five races are the best talkers, and he is also left to make up his own mind about which of these five is best. In making these choices, he has himself entered the seemingly irresolvable debate.

Sexing is a problem with the Yellow Fronted Amazons. As is the case in many other South American parrot species, there are no plumage differences between males and females.

Breeding Amazon Parrots

As with many of the other areas of the life cycle and behavior of *A. ochrocephala* which are currently unstudied and undocumented, the literature on the reproductive habits of the species leaves much to be desired for both captive and wild birds. With what information is available, however, a reasonable profile of the breeding habits of the species can be assembled. In general, since there are few essential differences between one subspecies and another aside from some minor physical features, it can be generally assumed that the egg size, nesting site, copulation frequency and other variables are similar among the subspecies. Hence, if there are some data, for example, concerning the copulatory pattern of the Single Yellow Head (*A. o. ochrocephala*) it can be generally assumed that all other subspecies will act similarly and that if there are differences among the subspecies, such differences will be for the most part insignificant in the over-all scheme of the reproductive process. However, there are differences in the personality structures of the various subspecies and their acceptance of captive conditions to the extent that one race may be more inclined to breed in captivity than others.

CHARACTERISTICS OF THE CLUTCH

Most written accounts reporting the number of eggs laid per clutch specify the usual number as being between three and five eggs. Usually, such reports are based on educated guesses and do not always reflect verification by actual field studies or examination of a captive breeding pair of *A. ochrocephala*. Given the data available—and there are a considerable number of reports providing an egg count—*a clutch of any number more than three should be considered unusual; the mean average clutch is between two and three eggs.*

The first written account of a clutch in the wild was reported by Colonel Grayson (1871). He found a nest of Tres Marias containing two eggs. At the turn of the century, the Beebes (1910) reported a clutch of three eggs with a newly hatched *A. o. ochrocephala* chick. Friedman and Smith (1950) had conducted at least two field studies in Venezuela, and they reported that the local residents had informed them that the average number of eggs per clutch was two. Later, in 1955, the same two researchers were given access to a Venezuelan breeder's notes of his *A.o. ochrocephala*. They found and reported that the Single Yellow-Headed pair had three consecutive nests each containing a clutch of three.

In captivity, a Double Yellow Headed male X Panama female crossing produced a clutch of one on the first try and a clutch of three the following year (Patrick, 1936). Belcher and Smooker (1936) reported that a captive pair of *A. o. ochrocephala* on the island of Trinidad had a clutch of three.

In recent captive breedings, Smith (1967) reported that his pair of Single Yellow Heads (*A. o. ochrocephala*) laid two infertile eggs during the spring of 1966 but that this unsuccessful nesting was followed in 1967 by the pair's raising two youngsters. (Smith did not disclose the number of eggs that the pair had laid.) Further, in another published article Smith (1970) reported the successful breeding of a pair of Double Yellow Heads (*A. o. oratrix*) that first laid two eggs in 1969 and then followed that clutch in the following year with four eggs. Both these breedings were in Great Britain.

In the United States Hensel (1977) had a pair which produced three eggs and successfully hatched two of them.

There are a few references in the literature concerning the size of eggs laid by *A. ochrocephala*, but a study of the reports makes it apparent that three of the four sources have drawn upon the fourth source for their data. Belcher and Smooker (1936) were first to report the size of the eggs from a pair of *A. o. ochrocephala;* the eggs were reported to be 40.2 x 30.4, 41 x 31.3 and 41.2 x 31 mm in size. (It is not clear whether the authors actually saw the eggs, whether these figures were published in an ornithological or avicultural publication or whether the authors had received the figures verbally from some undisclosed source, for they wrote "Three eggs laid in confinement . . ." and then proceeded to discuss the shape, color and size of the eggs.) Additionally, because there seems to be no other published account itemizing egg sizes, it is not clear whether the dimensions detailed by Belcher and Smooker are accurate representations of all subspecies of *A. ochrocephala* and whether, in fact, they are normal sized eggs for the species.

However, assuming that the authors measured the eggs themselves or that their source was reliable, there is no reason to seriously doubt the validity of the egg size of *A. ochrocephala* as given by them; as *A. o. ochrocephala* is an average-size subspecies, it would be reasonable to expect that the sizes published are relatively representative of all subspecies within the *A. ochrocephala* complex.

The eggs are white, ovate, glossy and, as reported by Herklots (1961), thick-shelled. Belcher and Smooker (1936) also observed that the eggs had "minute corrugations and scattered pittings."

BREEDING BEHAVIOR IN THE WILD

The distance between the most northerly range of *A. ochrocephala* and the most southerly range is several thousand kilometers, yet based on the existing evidence there does not appear to be a wide variation in the months in which the various subspecies breed and raise their young. From all the evidence, it appears that all of the subspecies breed very early in the year. On February 10, for example, Friedman and Smith (1950) collected a female *A. o. ochrocephala* which had enlarged gonads, and in March and April the same researchers were offered at various times nestlings and fledglings at different stages of development.

On the Las Tres Marias Islands *A. o. tresmariae* has a breeding season which begins in January, whereas on the Mexican mainland *A. o. oratrix* begins breeding in April and May (Grant 1966). Russel (1964) reported that in Belize eggs of *A. o. belizensis* were found during March and April and that during May a fledgling was found in a nest. I have on several occasions while travelling throughout Mexico, especially in the northern states, seen fledglings offered for sale during late May and early June. In most cases it was undeterminable whether the young birds were native to Mexico or had been smuggled from more southern countries in order to meet the tourist demand for inexpensive parrots. Dark-eyed young birds have been seen offered for sale as late as August, but such offerings are rare.

The nest of *A. ochrocephala* has been observed on occasion to be constructed out of a vacated termite nest (Friedman and Smith, 1950). Usually, however, nests are found in the hollows of trees (Grayson, 1871), the nesting cavity sometimes being several inches below the entrance. The final choice of nesting site appears to be determined by the type of trees found in the area. Sometimes the highest trees are chosen, sometimes not. Beebe and Beebe (1910), for example, described the nests as being in the "tops of the tallest, most inaccessible trees," yet the nest which they were themselves to investigate was only several feet from the ground. The report of Nelson (1899), by inference, would suggest that the Tres Marias chose nesting sites which were not too high above the ground, for in his discussion of the capture of young parrots, he noted how easy it was to get to the nest itself.

The Beebes reported the entrance to the nest as being rectangular, about three by six inches large, and the nest itself ". . . some five feet above the ground." They described the nest itself as being deep within a cavity in which the eggs were laid in a nest of chips. But Grayson (1871) examined a nest that "had been a little scooped out, forming a slight indentation," and that the eggs had been laid "upon the bare rotten wood."

BREEDING IN CAPTIVITY

Information concerning the breeding and rearing of *A. ochrocephala* in captivity is meager. While undoubtedly there have been some successful breedings in captivity involving most of the subspecies currently recognized, the absence of published data forces the serious student of aviculture to conclude that such breedings are rare, significantly rarer than the successes achieved by breeders of the African Grey (*Psittacus erithacus*).

The rarity of the species' breeding in captivity can perhaps be best measured by successes in England, where the British Avicultural Society has kept meticulous records for over a cen-

Hollow logs have been used as nest sites by some Amazons being bred in captivity.

tury. The same Clifford Smith mentioned a few pages ago was successful in breeding not only the Single Yellow Headed Amazon (*A. o. ochrocephala*) but also the Double Yellow Head (*A. o. oratrix*). These successes occurred in 1967 for *A. o. ochrocephala* and then in 1970 for *A. o. oratrix*. In both instances, the breedings were the first to be reported in Britain, and for both achievements Mr. Smith was awarded the Society's highest award for achievement. (See Editorial Inquiry, *Avicultural Magazine*, V. 73, 1967, p. 200 and *Avicultural Magazine*, V. 76, 1970, p. 235.)

However, since some success has been reported, it is apparent that the species will breed in captivity and, in certain instances (or so it would appear) as suggested by some published accounts, without any special encouragement by the breeder. One suspects that in the United States, particularly, *Amazona ochrocephala* is perceived more as a talking pet than a prospective parent. Also, given the easy accessibility to Mexican and Central American populations of the species, there is no urgency to develop breeding programs, because there are ample numbers of captured birds—both young and old—available to the public at relatively low cost. This situation will probably remain the same until public demand exceeds supply. The species reaches maturity at about five years of age, and sexual maturity sometimes shortly after, and since tamed parrots more frequently than not show little interest in breeding under the best of conditions, maintaining a small flock of the species for breeding purposes only could be an expensive venture for the average breeder, especially since the brood is small and there is no guarantee that the species will breed.

Given the lack of available data concerning the species' breeding habits and development, our current understanding of the various factors related to successful captive breeding is limited. Most of the available information, moreover, pertains to the breeding of the Single Yellow Head (*A. o. ochrocephala*), and while there is no reason to believe that there would be significant differences among the reproductive activities of the various subspecies, this belief has not yet been confirmed.

NESTING AND BROODING BEHAVIOR

In those reports which have become part of the established records in aviculture, there is almost always some mention of difficulties encountered during a pair's first courtship, mating behavior, nesting or rearing of the young. On a somewhat humorous note, for example, Hensel (1977) described the attempt of her cock Double Yellow Head (*A. o. oratrix*) to convince a hen that a family would be in her best interests. She wrote:

> Originally she was paired with a Double Yellow Head which drove her into the nest box. If she refused, he would knock her to the floor, bite her feet severely and drag her by the tail across the floor. I would not believe this was normal behavior.

This rather unfortunate and one-sided courtship was eventually ended when the beleaguered hen was paired with a more understanding cock. It is not quite clear from Mrs. Hensel's account, however, what eventually became of the overzealous suitor.

On a more serious note, however, that same hen had had two successful hatchings the two years preceding the unsuccessful mating attempt with the aggressive male. One chick hatched each time, but in both instances the youngsters were lost because of parental neglect. Similarly, Smith (1967, 1970) found that with both *A. o. oratrix* and *A. o. ochrocephala* pairs there was a clutch of eggs laid on the first nesting, but in both instances the eggs remained unhatched. Such problems are not necessarily indicative of detrimental traits within the species; the problems may indeed instead be related to the inexperience and immaturity of the nesting pair. It has long been an established fact that tamed parrots frequently fare poorly at breeding and nesting because captivity and domesticity have a tendency to dampen natural instincts.

Additionally, since the lack of sexual dimorphism in the species makes potential breeders difficult to sex (at least without resorting to surgical methods), the problem arises as to whether indeed there is true pair in the flight. Given that the species rarely shows interest in reproduction while in captivity, and the sexes are difficult to determine, a hopeful breeder may have placed together a "pair" which were in fact of the same sex. Such a breeder could never be certain, once the error was discovered, whether each of the individual birds would have been prepared to nest had a suitable mate been available. Needless to say, a great deal of time and energy will have been expended, and the breeder will have to begin anew.

When there is an actual pair and they are showing an interest in beginning a nest, their behavior is unmistakable. For example, Smith (1967) observed that whenever he approached the pair when they were perched in the flight, one of the pair always positioned itself between Smith and the mate. Smith found that that protective male ". . . had no hesitation in having a bite if my hands came too near."

Nesting interest and behavior in captivity generally follow the pattern of the species exhibited in the wild. Friedman and Smith (1955) found that the hen of a Venezuelan pair of *A. o. ochrocephala* began work on her nest within three days of the initial copulation. The work on the nest was sporadic, stretching over a month until the last copulation, and while it was the hen which did most of the nest-building, the cock was at times observed to assist. It should be noted that the pair had full liberty in the breeder's yard. Hensel (1977) reported that her *A. o. ochrocephala* individuals began showing an interest in nesting during April.

The interior of this aviary has been lined with wire to prevent damage from such ardent chewers of wood as Amazon parrots.

Smith's (1970) report mentioned a pair that began showing an interest in April; shortly after that the hen was observed excavating in the nest, throwing out various unwanted peat moss nesting materials placed there for her. By the end of the first week, the first egg was laid. Similarly, in a letter written to the editor of *Aviculture* in 1937, Leon Patrick reported that he had had a successful breeding of an *A. o. panamensis* X *A. o. ochrocephala* pair which had hatched an egg by June 3 and that subsequently the same pair had laid their first egg the following year by March 25.

Friedman and Smith (1955) were fortunate in their field studies in Venezuela in developing a friendship with a Venezuelan collector who permitted his pair of Single Yellow Heads complete freedom to raise their family as they chose. The collector (unnamed) had kept meticulous notes. He first received the pair in 1945 when they were nestlings, and it was not until 1951 that the pair first copulated and a clutch was laid. During the intervening six years their primaries had been clipped, and while the birds were frequently in the collector's home, they were at equal liberty in the trees surrounding the premises. The intervals between the first copulation and the laying of the clutch for three consecutive years were recorded as follows:

	First Copulation	Complete Clutch	Number of Eggs
1951	Feb. 25	Mar. 20	3
1952	Feb. 8	Mar. 25	3
1953	Feb. 10	Mar. 3	3

While there appear to be serious discrepancies between the various reports concerning when the clutch is laid, this differential can be accounted for by the climatic zones in which the successful breedings take place. The breeding instincts of parrots are governed by the length of daylight hours and temperature. The Earth's temperate zones afford the appropriate conditons at dates in the year different from those provided by tropical and semi-tropical zones.

The facilities provided the breeding pair are, as would be expected, large. Hensel (1977) provided her pair of Double Yellow-Heads with a caged area 8 feet long by 6 feet wide. (Unfortunately she provided no additional information concerning the nesting facilities themselves.) Smith's facilities (1970) were substantially larger: a flight which was 12 feet long by 6 feet wide by 7 feet high and which had connected to it an auxiliary 6 feet by 4 feet room which the pair could use as a shelter in inclement weather. His facilities (1967) for the *A. o. ochrocephala* pair were only slightly smaller.

The grandfather clock type of nesting box was found more acceptable to nesting pairs (Smith, 1970) than hollow logs. Smith originally provided his pairs with hollowed logs, but with no success. He surmised that the logs presented a problem for the birds because they provided the hen and her eggs no protection from the weather. The grandfather clock type nesting box which was used to replace the hollowed log was 5 feet high by 10 inches square. It had a four-inch entrance hole cut approximately six inches from the top. The actual nest bottom was approximately a foot down from the entrance. The floor was covered with a layer of peat moss and turf. A bit of wire mesh was nailed to the inside of the box so that the hen could easily climb in and out. The top of the nesting box had a glass top securely fastened to it.

THE NESTLINGS

Incubation begins after the first egg has been laid, and the full clutch usually is completed by the end of the first week after the first egg has been laid. The female alone incubates. During the entire incubation period she is fed by the cock at the nest via regurgitation (French, 1973) but when the hen is outside the nest she may feed herself. Usually, however, the female will be seen begging food even when she may be standing beside a plate of food (Friedman and Smith, 1955). During incubation, the male remains near the nest, but he has not been observed to enter it except to feed the female. The hen sits tight and constant, leaving the nest for only brief periods (Smith, 1967).

The incubation period is the usual 28 days. With his *A. o. oratrix*, Smith (1967) observed that the first egg was laid on May 7, with the first sounds of young being heard coming on June 5.

There is some confusion concerning the natal down of the young chicks. Some reports testify that it is gray, while others say that it is white. Beebe and Beebe (1910), for example, after finding

Unfortunately, this Double Yellow Head egg, from a clutch of two, did not hatch. The other egg did hatch, and the chick was taken from the nest to be hand-fed.

This seven-week-old Double Yellow Head has been successfully hand-raised.

an *A. o. ochrocephala* nest in the wild, broke into it to find three eggs and an infant with white natal down.

The extremely young birds are apparently quite sensitive to environmental changes, for the Beebes observed that a newly hatched youngster which was lying motionless in the shade would move if sunlight struck it. During such movement it kept up a "continuous, low, raucous cry like the mew of a catbird."

Brooding of the young continues faithfully until about three weeks before they are prepared to leave the nest. At approximately seven weeks of age the young birds are fully feathered (Patrick, 1936), although their overall green appearance reflects their immaturity: the yellow is not as pronounced on the crown, the eyes are a full brownish black color with the pupil undiscernible, and there is little coloration, if any, on the bend of the wing.

When the young have left the nest, they are fully capable of feeding themselves, but it has been observed that they will continue to beg food from the parents for as long as the adults are prepared to feed them.

DIET FOR NESTING PAIRS

No doubt the diet offered the parents and young will vary depending on availability of particular foods and on breeders' convictions as to what best suits the needs of a growing family and the continued maintenance of health in the adults. Smith (1967) has used a diet which has proved successful not only with *A. o. ochrocephala* but also with the African Greys *(Psittacus erithacus)* which he has successfully bred. The brooding pair are given a mixture of seeds which includes millet, canary seeds, sunflower, oats, wheat and safflower. Since the breeding birds show a distinct preference for pre-soaked seeds, an ample portion is scattered over the flight floor. Dry seeds are also provided for the pairs, but they are the last foods to be eaten. (The parents eventually again developed a preference for the dry seeds, but this occurred only during the last week of brooding.)

In addition to the seeds, various fruits and greens were amply supplied the parrots each day: dandelion roots and leaves, groundsel and sow thistle in addition to the usual fruits. Smith (1970) found that while fruits were offered, the brooding parents ate the fruit only after the presoaked seeds and greens were no longer available.

DIET OF CAGED PET YELLOW FRONTS

The diet provided most caged Yellow Fronts, regardless of subspecies, is for the most part not only generally unsatisfactory and inadequate but also potentially injurious to the parrots' health. Most parrot owners, regrettably, rely on a heavy diet of safflower, sunflower and peanuts, often to the total exclusion of other and more nutritious foods. This over-reliance on seeds would not be so much a health problem if it were not for the fact that caged parrots are not afforded sufficient exercise.

These seeds, which are almost always enjoyed by *A. ochrocephala*, have a very high fat content. Because of the lack of sufficient exercise, the caged parrot begins developing a serious case of fat buildup of the arteries and veins in the heart area, leading to premature heart attacks. *It should be emphasized that, in the wild, seeds play only a minor role in the daily diet of A. ochrocephala.*

One of several different styles of parrot stands, a very useful accessory for those times when the pet parrot is out of its cage.

The caged *A. ochrocephala* almost always also receives an inadequate vitamin intake in its daily food offerings, because it is usually not given an adequate supply of fruits and greens. Because most people have at least a vague awareness of nutritional needs (and if they don't their pet dealers will almost always recommend a bottle of liquid vitamins to be included in the parrot sale), the owner of an *A. ochrocephala* invariably attempts to compensate for the lack of adequate vitamins from the proper diet by introducing bottled vitamins into the bird's water dish.

But not all parrots enjoy water, and for those that do occasionally enjoy a drink, the water intake may be too infrequent to compensate for the daily deprivation of vitamins needed for prime health. In short, it is unfortunate but true that a significant pro-

The intake of fatty seeds such as sunflower (left), which form the basis of many parrot diets, should be adjusted to the need of the captive parrot, which likely gets little exercise. Fruits such as apple (below) should always form a portion of a pet parrot's diet.

portion of *A. ochrocephala* owners expose their caged pets to malnutrition and various health problems resulting from a continuously inadequate diet!

In feeding our birds we take great pains to ensure that each individual bird receives as balanced a food intake as might be expected if the bird were in the wilds, where its instincts would dictate its feeding habits.

While any given individual *A. ochrocephala* may reject the various kinds of foods which are forced into its diet because of its own personal likes and dislikes, every Yellow Front in the author's care eventually has been exposed to the following greens: cauliflower, Brussels sprouts, peas, cabbage, radish and celery leaves, raw potatoes, dandelion leaves and roots, eucalyptus leaves, fresh corn and broccoli. There are probably other vegetables and greens which could be successfully introduced into the parrot's diet; of course, the availability of many types of nutritious greens is subject to seasonal and geographic variations. Usually, however, any Yellow Front which we have had for two or more weeks, regardless of its former eating habits and stubbornness, will learn to relish at least three or more different greens in that period. Some parrots have developed such a taste for seeds while in captivity, particularly in after-quarantine holding stations and pet stores, that they seem virtually impossible to change. This problem can be overcome, however.

The same can be said of fruits. Our Yellow Fronts receive bananas, apples, grapes, oranges, cherries, peaches and whatever other fruits and berries may be readily available at a given time. Because apples, oranges and grapes are almost always available, they generally form the mainstay of the fruit portion of our birds' diets. Given the wide diversity of fruits and berries available in different geographical regions, however, the list of different fruits and berries which the species will readily accept is far more extensive.

In addition, sunflower, safflower, peanuts, pine nuts, wheat, pecans and walnuts are offered the parrots. Seeds, however, never form a greater part than one-third of the bird's daily food intake. We are particularly parsimonious in giving the parrots seeds which are noted for their fat content—peanuts, oats and safflower.

Although some Amazons at first refuse to eat anything except seeds, vegetables such as broccoli (left) and corn (below), and fruits should be included in their diet.

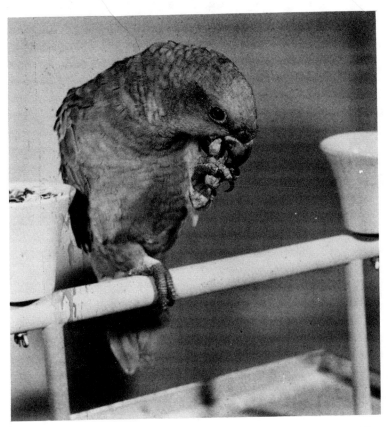

This young Yellow Nape is eating a favorite treat, a peanut. No more than one-third of an Amazons' daily diet should be seeds, and peanuts and other seeds which contain a lot of fat should be provided sparingly.

Naturally, not all of these foods find their way into each food dish each day. What is normally fed is dictated by what is generally in the refrigerator each day. Since fruit and vegetable shopping is frequent, there is always a variety of different fruits and vegetables available at any given time. Once the personality of a given bird is established and its likes and dislikes determined, each bird's diet is then, of course, somewhat tailored to meet that particular bird's specific personal preferences. There is no bird, however, which is permitted to retain an absolute preference for seeds and a total rejection of greens and vegetables.

Double Yellow Headed Amazon, *A. o. oratrix*. Because its home range lies so near to the United States, the Double Yellow Head is one of the most commonly available Amazons.

The Subspecies of
Amazona ochrocephala

AMAZONA OCHROCEPHALA ORATRIX (RIDGWAY)

A. o. oratrix is commonly called any one of a variety of popular names: Double Yellow, Yellow Head, Mexican Double Yellow Head and, at times, it is still referred to as Levaillant's Amazon, an archaic term now rarely used although it was popular last century.

Physical Dimensions of *A.o. oratrix*:

	Wing	Tail	Culmen	Tarsus
Males	217-245mm	108-136mm	31-37mm	24-27mm
Females	212-240mm	105-126.5mm	30-36mm	23-26mm

Physical Description

The Double Yellow Head is frequently confused with the Tres Marias Amazon *(A. o. tresmariae)*. The two subspecies are quite similar in appearance, so it is understandable that the two should be confused, even by advanced aviculturists. There are, however, noticeable differences between them; the differences become immediately obvious even to the uninitiated when the two are placed side by side.

The Double Yellow Head has somewhat less yellow in head coverage than the Tres Marias. Its yellow does not extend as far down the throat area adjoining the upper breast. Also, unlike *A. o. tresmariae,* whose yellow coverage may include the entire back of the neck area, even infringing on the back region, the yellow of *A. o. oratrix* is restricted to the hindneck area. On *A. o. oratrix* this yellow is deeper and brighter than that on *A. o. tresmariae.*

There are color differences on both back and breast feathers as well. The breast feathers on *A. o. oratrix* are best described as approximating a faint yellowish green, whereas the back feathers are a distinct parrot green. *A. o. tresmariae* has breast feathers having a bluish tinge to them, and the back feathers are considerably darker, sometimes referred to as an "oil green" color.

Finally, some mature *A. o. tresmariae* specimens will have minute scatterings of red feathering in the lower reaches of the yellow head coloring in the throat area. *A. o. tresmariae* is a slightly larger bird and more massive appearing than *A. o. oratrix.*

HEAD: As noted above, the yellow head coverage on *A. o. oratrix* includes all portions of the head, extending downwards on the underside to include the throat and foreneck and on the dorsal side as far down as to include the hindneck. The forehead and crown yellow pigmentation is a slightly lighter hue than that found on the ear coverts, lores, cheeks and chin. The lower regions are a darker shade yet.
The beak is horn colored, the iris orange.

BODY: The Double Yellow Head's back is a typical parrot green, but the feathers of the sides, chest and breast are decidedly lighter colored in a yellow to a yellowish green tone. This lighter shade extends down the underside of the body to include the upper abdominal region.

WINGS: The bend of the wing consists of a mixture of both yellow and poppy red feathers, with the red predominating. The carpal edge is a bright yellow. The upper wing coverts tend towards a yellowish green. The first four secondaries are a bright poppy red for the greater part of the feather except for the extreme end of the covered basal part, which is yellow. The terminal portion changes from a yellow to violet blue. The primaries are parrot green at the basal portion but are a violet blue at the distal half.

TAIL: The distal portions of the tail tend to be a bright yellowish green, with the remaining portions of the green feathers a standard parrot green. The upper tail coverts are distinctly yellowish green. The outer four feathers on each side have poppy red webs on their inner side, phasing into a yellow at the basal portion.

FEET: The inner thighs are yellowish green, similar to but lighter than the chest and breast hues, while the outer thighs are a darker parrot green. The legs and feet are a grayish color.

IMMATURES: Extremely young individuals have yellow restricted to the lores, forehead and crown. With adolescents, the yellow covers most of the head, but the coloration does not extend as far downwards on the hindneck. The yellow on the front lower portion of the head includes only the chin. But by the time the bird is two or so years old, much of the throat and/or foreneck will also be yellow.

The bend of the wing is primarily green, but it may have some hint of red and yellow to it. The carpal edge is a yellowish green. The eyes of the very young are dark brown.

Geographical Distribution

The Mexican Double Yellow Head enjoys an extensive range over a significant portion of the land mass of Mexico. The subspecies was at first considered to have a more northerly range which extended as far north as the Rio Grande, the river which forms the major part of the international boundary between Mexico and the United States. Salvin (1871) had made this assumption based on a specimen collected in 1857 and then again later, on another collected in 1859. Evidence drawn from subsequent field studies, however, revealed that the subspecies' most northerly range is along the Caribbean slope in the northern states of Tamulipas and Nuevo Leon. At its most northern and western limits, the subspecies includes all of the Atlantic slope in Nuevo Leon, and its most northerly extension along the slope is to the central region of Tamaulipas.

A. o. oratrix occupies the entire eastern Atlantic slope stretching southward to include all of Vera Cruz. It is not found on the northern portions of the plateau in central Mexico, although it does range northward in the central part of Mexico to include the state of Guanajuato.

Its most westerly extension of range is found in the southern portions of Mexico, where it extends westward as far as the

Map of the geographic distribution of *A. o. oratrix*.

eastern borders of Colima. Colima, in that respect, also serves as the most northerly extent of range along the Pacific coastal region. The subspecies extends as far south along the Pacific coast as to include the states of Guerrero, Oaxaca and Chiapas in the far south. Chiapas forms the most southerly extent of the range, meeting the most northerly limit of the Yellow Nape *(A. o. auropalliata)*.

During the previous century, there was considerable speculation that the range of *A.o. oratrix* also included the Caribbean regions of Yucatan and Belize. Salvin (1866), for example, found that *A. ochrocephala* was common as a caged bird in Belize. He was led to conclude, therefore, that the subspecies was native to both Yucatan and Belize. Subsequent field studies have shown that the most southerly range of the subspecies along the Atlantic coast does not extend far enough southwards and eastwards as to include these areas, and Monroe and Howell (1966) after considerable field work, defined the indigenous subspecies common to Belize as a separate subspecies, *A.o. belizensis*.

While *A.o. oratrix* does not range into the northern portions of Mexico along the Pacific coast, it is believed that at some past time it may have indeed extended as far northwards as the city of Mazatlan.

A.O. ORATRIX AS A PET

The Double Yellow Head has for many decades remained a staple in the exotic bird pet trade. The legends prevailing about its prowess as a talker, its attractive plumage, its colorful behavior, its ready accessibility and reasonable price compared to other parrots make it a perennial favorite, and this popularity persists despite the unfavorable opinions held by some aviculturists and advanced bird fanciers.

Those who hold reservations concerning this bird's desirability rarely challenge the authenticity of the kinds of desirable attributes mentioned above; rather, their chief complaint involves the trait of unpredictability. When considering *A.o. oratrix* and its trait of unpredictability, a matter which will be discussed shortly, it must be remembered that there are three species of parrots *(A. ochrocephala, A. aestiva* and *P. erithacus)* which surpass all other species of parrots and parrot types in talkability. These three species have a combined total of fourteen subspecies among them. *A. o. oratrix* ranks in the top three or four in talkability of all these subspecies. Probably for that reason alone, *A.o. oratrix* continues to retain its popularity among bird fanciers. Like all of the other subspecies of the three best talkers, *A. o. oratrix* demonstrates time and time again that it deserves its reputation even though there are many individual birds within the subspecies which are totally undesirable.

The problem of unpredictability relates to two fundamental qualities desirable in any species of talking parrot: its tamability as a pet and its propensity to talk. In speaking of the bird's unpredictability, discussion does not concern itself with the characteristic of many species of parrots and parrot types to develop an intense loyalty to one person and an intense dislike for all others; rather, the unpredictability referred to here relates to the problem of the bird's personality. There is frankly no sure way of assuring that a bronco *oratrix* can be tamed and developed into a pet which enjoys human companionship.

Most species of birds are recognized for various characteristics which may or may not be desirable, and while individual birds within a given species may deviate from the norm, usually there is a degree of reliability in predicting the relationship between bird and man. As a case in point, the African Grey Parrot *(Psittacus erithacus)* is a good example. While the species is noted for a diversity of favorable and unfavorable qualities, there are three characteristics concerning its personality which stand out: the excellence of its mimicry, its easy tamability and its 'standoffishness.' Exceptions exist, but by and large, when an African Grey is purchased, the purchaser can expect the following: a parrot which will be readily and easily tamed, which will tolerate people but will not accept friendship with ease, and which will generally talk well and be able to imitate several different kinds of voices.

With the Double Yellow Head, however, this kind of assuredness does not exist. The parrot may become a pet, a bird which is absolutely adorable in its relationship with people and absolutely trustworthy. But then, too, the closest relationship that it may accept with humans is a bare tolerance of them; worse still, it may not accept any type of taming, let alone tolerance or intimacy. There is just no way of predicting the odds which will be favorable for the pet owner.

One could raise the issue of the preferability of immature specimens. It is a general rule of thumb, a rule which could even be described as an axiom, that the younger the specimen, the greater the positive results that can be expected from the parrot. But this rule cannot be applied to the Double Yellow Head with any great assurance. A fledgling may be absolutely delightful, a real 'pet,' but upon maturity it may become cantankerous, irritable and prone to bite frequently and unpredictably.

The second major area of unpredictability relates, unfortunately, to one of the qualities for which it is internationally recognized—its talkability. Not all individuals within the subspecies known for their proclivity to talk actually talk. Some never talk. Some talk better than others. But, by and large, there is a degree of predictability about a given bird from a specific species concerning its talkability. If we buy an African Grey, we can for the most part reliably expect that that bird will talk; we may be disappointed at first, but the chances are that it will eventually perform to expectations. If we purchase a Green Cheeked Amazon *(Amazona viridigenalis)*, the odds are that the specimen will never utter a word beyond a shriek, but we might be delightfully surprised to find that it becomes an accomplished mimic.

A.o. oratrix does not offer this kind of predictability, however. But when the Double Yellow Head talks, it is unexcelled. The talkers generally acquire extensive vocabularies, often with what seems a minimal amount of training. When it does not talk, on the other hand, its failure to do so is almost always absolute.

These two areas of unpredictability, unfortunately, lead to a third concern. Some people really don't care whether their parrots become accomplished talkers or not, so long as they are 'good' pets. Others care less whether a parrot is a good pet or not, so long as its mimicry can be a source of amusement and pleasure. Most bird fanciers, however, want a parrot which is both a talker *and* a pet. Getting both qualities in a Double Yellow Head can be a risky gamble. The problem would not be so exaggerated if predictability

Young chicks can readily be taught to feed from a spoon.

could reasonably assure us that *A.o. oratrix* will at least tolerate the human presence. The parrot is just as likely to prove to be a biter as a tame pet bird.

There is no question about it, however; a "good" Double Yellow Head is an unexcelled parrot. In addition to the positive qualities earlier described "good" Double Yellow Headed Amazons can prove to be gentle and extremely colorful in their behavior, the latter characteristic lacking in most other subspecies of the three best talking parrot species. In my book *Taming and Training Parrots*, I described the behavior of my pet two-year-old *A. o. oratrix*:

> Having a hanging cage with ropes dangling from it to within a few inches from the floor, Selsa occupies herself for hours by climbing from ceiling to floor, doing all sorts of acrobatics, acting silly, amusing herself.

That particular *oratrix* can only be described as an absolute darling, although by the end of her second year she had on three occasions revealed the unpredictability factor common to her race by biting three different people on different occasions for no apparent reason whatever. Even given this fault, she was for the most part trustworthy and absolutely loyal to her masters, following them throughout the house should she be left alone in a room. For Selsa, happiness was a shoulder, and as I wrote: "Should we take her to the beach or to a swap meet, she is just as content to sit on the shoulder for several hours."

Additionally, the species has long been recognized for its extreme hardiness, as compared to many other species which do poorly in captivity. As early as the mid-nineteenth century, this quality was recognized in the subspecies and put into good use in Britain, where large estate owners would release numbers into the woods on their lands. The birds were expected to survive the winter, and they did! Their greatest danger seemed to be the hunters who could not resist the temptation of shooting these colorful foreigners out of the skies (Greene, 1884).

Similarly, John Bull, as noted earlier, provided excellent illustration of the hardiness and adaptability of *A. o. oratrix* when he reported that two of them had survived New York's usual bitter winters by eating crabapples.

There is no question about the Double Yellow Head's hardiness. In most regions of the United States, if properly acclimated by being put outdoors during the summer, most birds could probably survive quite well year in and year out outdoors.

Finally, if provided a proper diet and reasonable health care, *A. o. oratrix* can be expected to live a long time. Specimens which are forty, fifty and more years old are by no means uncommon. Reasonable care of *A. o. oratrix* does not necessitate or include pampering or special attention.

Even given its unpredictability, *A. o. oratrix* is one of the best choices for a talking parrot. While disappointment may be suffered in choosing a given specimen, once the right bird has been found   there will be no question concerning the Double Yellow Head's international reputation.

Double Yellow Heads are unpredictable in regard to their tamability and talkability. Here a Cockatiel snatches a few seeds from a Double Yellow Head's food dish.

AMAZONA OCHROCEPHALA TRESMARIAE (NELSON)

A. o. tresmariae was first classified as a subspecies by E.W. Nelson in 1900. It is popularly called the Tres Marie or the Tres Maria, and sometimes simply the Tres. More frequently than not, because of its similarity to the Mexican Double Yellow Head *(A. o. oratrix)*, it is mistakenly referred to as a Double Yellow Head.

Physical Dimensions of A. o. tresmariae:

	Wing	Tail	Culmen	Tarsus
Males	225-245mm	121-140mm	32-34.5mm	24-27mm
Females	226-237mm	130-136mm	30-32mm	24.5-26mm

Physical Description

The Tres Marias is so similar to the Mexican Double Yellow Head that the two subspecies are frequently confused, with the names being used interchangeably. This confusion is not limited to lay persons. Quite frequently the mistake in identification is made by both aviculturists and dealers in livestock alike. Bates and Busenbark (1978) relate an incident in which

> The writers know of one whose toenails they have trimmed at regular intervals for several years. It is by far the most beautiful "Yellow Head" they have ever seen. The owner has no idea that it is a far more rare bird than the Mexican Double Yellow Head.

While the similarities are striking, the differences become especially apparent if the two subspecies are compared side by side. *A.o. tresmariae* is a somewhat larger bird, more stocky in appearance. Its appearance of being larger than the Double Yellow Head *(A.o. oratrix)* is exaggerated by the slightly larger tail that *A.o. tresmariae* possesses.

There are some differences in coloration. *A.o. tresmariae* has more yellow to the head, with the yellow extending to (and sometimes including the upper portions of) foreneck and upper back. In all cases, the head and neck are completely yellow. The yellow coloration is also less bright and intense than in the Double Yellow Head.

A.o. tresmariae has a decidedly bluish tinge to its breast plumage, whereas that of the Double Yellow Head is clearly a yellowish green hue. The back is more an 'oil green' tone than the parrot green characterizing the back of *A.o. oratrix*.

HEAD: As noted above, the head is entirely yellow, with the yellow covering the crown, forehead, occiput and lores and extending downwards to include the hindneck and throat regions. On the dorsal side, the yellow may extend downwards into the upper regions of the back. Like the adults of *A. o. oratrix*, mature *A. o. tresmariae* adults may have flecks of red randomly but sparingly flecked throughout the lowest area of yellow bordering the green of the back and breast.

The iris in *A. o. tresmariae* is orange, and the beak, which is somewhat broader than the Double Yellow Head's, is horn colored.

BODY: The Tres Maria's side, breast and chest feathers are a bluish tinged green hue, more the tone of an emerald green. The back feathers are a slightly lighter shade of parrot green, an oil green.

WINGS: Like *A. o. oratrix*, the Tres Marie has a poppy colored red bend, flecked with yellow. The carpal edge is a bright yellow. The first four secondaries are bright poppy red; at the basal portion they are yellowish. There is a gradual change from yellow to violet blue in the terminal portions. The basal portions of the primaries are green, but the distal portions turn to a violet blue.

TAIL: The outer tail coverts are a somewhat yellowish green, a modest contrast to the lighter oil green of the back. There is a yellowish green hue to the distal portions of the tail feathers, while the remainder approximate the lighter oil green of the back. The inner webs of the outer four feathers on both sides are poppy red, gradually phasing at the final basal section into a yellow with a hint of green to it.

FEET: The legs and feet are a grayish flesh color. The lower extremes of thigh feathers, the booties, may be yellow.

IMMATURES: Immature Tres Marias look like the young of the Double Yellow Head. The head yellow does not extend any farther than the chin on the front and no farther than the upper neck on the back.

There is little if any red to the bend of the wing, although there may be some yellow flecks there. The carpal edge is a yellowish green. The iris is dark brown.

Note: Usually, when people claim they have a Tres Marias, they have in fact a Double Yellow Head. When buying an immature *A. o. tresmariae,* one should know the exact origin of the bird.

Geographical Distribution

A.o. tresmariae is limited geographically to the islands of Maria Madre, Maria Magdelena, Maria Cleofos and San Juanito off the Pacific coast of Mexico. This group of four islands is known collectively as the Tres Marias Islands; they are situated approximately 21°—22° North latitude by 106°—107° West longitude and are approximately 200 km. S.S.W. of Mazatlan and approximately 125 km. west of Nayarit, Mexico.

Because of the similarity in appearance of *A.o. tresmariae* to *A.o. oratrix* and the failure to draw distinctions between the two subspecies, there was an understandable effect on the attempt to define the exact range of the different subspecies of *A. ochrocephala.* For example, while Colonel Grayson (1871) had not found *A.o. oratrix* in Mazatlan, he described the Amazon parrots on the Islands as "peculiar to the Islands." Whether he was, in fact, identifying *A. ochrocephala* on the Tres Marias Islands as a distinct subspecies is not clear, for he wrote further that "It is not uncommon in southwest Mexico . . . it also inhabits middle and eastern Mexico."

In 1899, however, almost thirty years after the Grayson paper was published, Nelson was to write that "Colonel Grayson supposed these birds [to be peculiar to the Tres Marias, as he did not chance to] find them on the mainland. In reality, they are widely distributed on both coasts of Mexico." The problem that emerged is obvious: if the subspecies found on the Tres Marias was indeed simply an *A.o. oratrix,* then *A.o. oratrix* had a much larger geographical range than was previously believed; if, however, the bird found on the Islands was in truth "peculiar to the islands" and hence by implication different, then the range of *A.o. oratrix* stood as before, but a new subspecies would have been acknowledged. Nelson chose the former alternative, thereby giving *A.o. oratrix* a much larger range than is presently recognized.

Such difficulties may seem a typically trivial matter that only academics would find an interest in. But the problem is not as trivial as it first appears. If the island representataives of *A. ochrocephala* are indeed *A.o. oratrix,* how do we account for the differences which can be seen between the island representatives and their mainland counterparts? Whether or not they are a subspecies or simply a western population of *A.o. oratrix,* what does their habitation on the islands tell us about the evolutionary history of the species, the geological history of the region and similar concerns? The mere difference or similarity of birds separated by several hundred kilometers provides considerable insights into the various historical forces which have shaped the world as we understand it today.

For the reader's interest, Nelson (1900) later did an about face, recognizing the Tres Marias birds as a distinct subspecies of *A. ochrocephala,* and was subsequently credited with its discovery.

Whatever the case, since *A.o. oratrix* does not range as far west as Nayarit (indeed, its most immediate westerly point is considerably south of Nayarit and only as far west as the eastern boundaries of the state of Colima), there has been considerable speculation concerning the evolution of *A.o. oratrix* and *A.o. tresmariae.*

Evidence suggests that in the distant past the range of *A. ochrocephala* extended across northern Mexico as far west as to include the Tres Marias Islands and as far north along the Pacific coast as to at least San Juanito Island, the most northerly island in the Tres Marias group. The Tres Marias chain, according to present thinking, was probably not a chain of small islands separated from the peninsula to the south and the mainland to the east, but rather an extension of the regions now forming the states of Jalisco and Nayarit.

As a result of geological upheavals during the course of that region's geological history, a considerable portion of the Earth's crust sank below the ocean, leaving the higher levels of what now constitutes the Tres Marias Islands isolated by wide expanses of ocean from the mainland. During these geological convulsions,

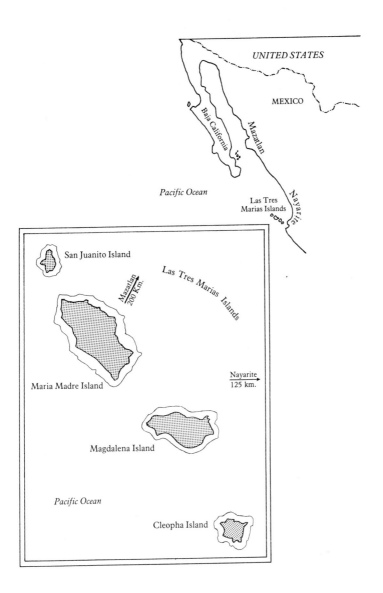

Map of the geographic distribution of *A. o. tresmariae.*

the islands may even have been thrust out of the sea, for such convulsions take place over countless centuries.

Representatives of *A. ochrocephala* on the Tres Marias Islands were thereby permanently isolated from the mainland population. During the thousands of years which followed, this isolation led to the evolution of the characteristics unique to *A. ochrocephala tresmariae*. It should be pointed out that there is almost no variation of plumage coloration or physical characteristics in the *A.o. oratrix* population throughout its entire mainland range and there is therefore nowhere to be found in native mainland populations of *A.o. oratrix* the characteristics common to *A.o. tresmariae*.

Stager (1957) postulates that over the centuries following the geological upheaval *A. ochrocephala* retreated from its more northerly range along the western coast of Mexico until it reached what is now its current range, considerably south of the Tres Marias Islands.

THE TRES MARIAS AMAZON AS A PET

Because of the limited territory available to this subspecies of *A. ochrocephala*, the Tres Marias Amazon is a much rarer bird and is not as frequently available to the pet trade as compared with the Double Yellow Head. *A.o. tresmariae* therefore commands a somewhat higher price than its mainland counterpart.

As a talker, *A.o. tresmariae* ranks in the top five or so of the races in the three best-known talking species. While there are few testimonials to draw upon as evidence of this subspecies' desirability as a pet and its proficiency at mimicry, it has been my experience that *A.o. tresmariae* is probably a better candidate for a pet than *A.o. oratrix*.

As noted earlier, one of the common characteristics of some subspecies within the *A. ochrocephala* complex is their colorful personality coupled with unpredictability, depending on the individual specimen. *A.o. tresmariae* tends to be a more "reliable" subspecies than *A.o. oratrix,* its main competitor in the pet trade for "Yellow Heads." It has been this writer's experience that *A.o. tresmariae* is less prone to become excited and generally proves to be more sedate and docile. Mention has already been made of this subspecies' docility in the wilds, where it proved easy to catch

A Double Yellow Head, *A. o. oratrix*. The Tres Marias Amazon, *A. o. tresmariae*, is often confused with the Double Yellow Head.

them simply by slipping a noose over their heads from the end of a long pole. Adults are generally easily tamed, although, because of their experience and maturity, they may be more "set in their ways" and therefore less inclined to enter a relationship with humans that could be termed a reciprocal relationship.

As is true of the Mexican Double Yellow Head, there are no general rules which would prove useful in choosing a particular specimen which will prove to be a good talker; there can be no general assurance that an individual *A.o. tresmariae* will talk.

When a Tres Marias Amazon does talk or mimic the variety of sounds that daily enter its life, however, it invariably proves to be proficient and generally accumulates an extensive vocabulary. During a visit to a home housing a Tres Marias, I rang the doorbell a few times but had to stand on the porch waiting (for what seemed the longest time) for someone to answer the door. Suddenly from inside could be heard a bedlam, indicating a great deal of excitement. As it turned out, the lady of the house had three teenaged daughters, and when the doorbell rang the first time, one of the young ladies yelled out, "There's someone at the door. I'll get it." Only a few seconds later their Tres Marias imitated exactly those sentences, in the exact tone of voice and volume. The parrot had just begun learning to talk three or four months earlier and had got into the habit of repeating complete sentences at times after hearing them but once.

Most Amazon parrots respond well to taming. This is a Yellow Nape, *A. o. auropalliata*.

AMAZONA OCHROCEPHALA BELIZENSIS
(MONROE AND HOWELL)

A.o. belizensis, rare in the United States, is popularly called the "Yellow Head" in Belize.

Physical dimensions of A.o. belizensis: The following figures provided for the dimensions of the *A.o. belizensis* were drawn from the original study by Monroe and Howell, 1966.

	Wing	Tail	Culmen	Tarsus
Males	211.5-220mm	116-120.5mm	31.2-33.5mm	33.3-35.6mm
Females	202.5mm	106.5m	31.5mm	32.9mm

Physical Description

A.o. belizensis was designated a subspecies by Burt Monroe and Thomas Howell in 1966. There are virtually no studies reporting the species from the Belize area prior to the Monroe and Howell expedition, which was the first to systematically collect specimens. There have been no subsequent follow-up field expeditions in the area, and there are no photographs known existing of this isolated and basically unstudied subspecies. (The author was fortunate in having the opportunity of discussing the species with Dr. Thomas Howell. As far as Dr. Howell was aware, the Monroe and Howell field study during 1966 was the last study to do documentary work on the subspecies.)

The one written documentation identifying and describing the physical characteristics of *A.o. belizensis* is the original Monroe and Howell study of 1966. The following description is taken verbatim from that study:

> . . . smaller size in all dimensions and reduced amount of yellow on the head of adults, this color is usually confined to the forehead, crown (extending posteriorly on crown to about level of eye), lores and auriculars, occasionally with a few scattered yellow feathers on throat and posterior crown. Differs from the more geographically remote *A.o. oratrix* (Ridgway) of western Mexico,

only in the color characters mentioned above (Monroe and Howell, 1966).

Geographical Distribution

A.o. belizensis is common only to the country of Belize; it is confined, as far as is presently known, to the lowland pine savanna. As an interesting corollary, while *A.o. oratrix* was originally considered to have an extended range which included both the Yucatan Peninsula and Guatemala (Salvin, 1866), it was subsequently found that its most southerly extension along the Caribbean is in the Mexican state of Veracruz. That small, isolated populations may be found in remote areas of Yucatan always remains a possibility, but no specimens have yet been collected in the region for the past century. The fact that the range of *A.o. oratrix* does not appear to extend into the region provides interesting research possibilities for explaining the isolation of *A.o. belizensis.*

Belize is a small country occupying approximately 9000 square miles and having a population of 100,000 or so. The distance separating *A.o. belizensis* from *A.o. oratrix* populations is approximately 400 miles. In 1964 Russel limited the range of *A.o. ochrocephala* in Belize to the Ycacos and Hill Bank lagoons and to an area approximately twenty miles south at the Sibun and Sitte rivers (Russel, 1964).

Other Information:

Russel's 1964 field research included a description of some of the subspecies' behavior in the wild. He observed that *A.o. belizensis* preferred the pine tree *Pinus caribaea* for their nests and roosting areas. Feeding, however, normally took place in the humid forests. During roosting, *A.o. belizensis* normally chose the highest branches of a tree, in which one or two pairs per tree could be found.

There is little more information concerning the species in the wild, except for some brief details concerning their reproductive cycles. In a female specimen that Russel collected in February the female carried an ovum 5mm in diameter. Later, during May, when Douglas Lancaster, an associate of Russel's, collected a male, the bird's testes were described as "enlarged" (Russel, 1964).

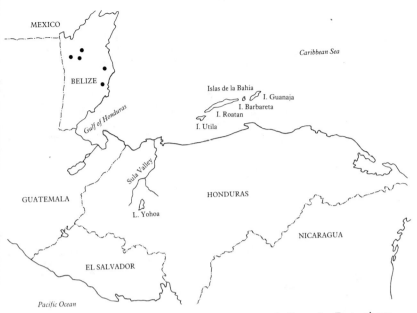

Map of the geographic distribution of *A. o. belizensis*. Dots show where specimens have been collected.

A.O. BELIZENSIS AS A PET

Outside Belize there is little known about the subspecies' characteristics as a pet. It could be generally assumed, however, that *A.o. belizensis's* behavior as a pet closely approximates, if it is not identical to, that of the Mexican Double Yellow Head *(A.o. oratrix)* or Tres Marias *(A.o. tresmariae)*.

Some observations have been made of the race as a caged bird in Belize, however. Salvin had visited the territory in 1866 and then again in 1871 and noted that ". . . it may frequently be seen as a cage-bird" (Salvin, 1871). Russel was to describe *A.o. belizensis* as the 'personal yellow head' (Russel, 1964). One could conclude that the little evidence there is suggests that *A.o. belizensis* is a popular household parrot and, judging from Russel's choice of adjective, a pleasant parrot.

It is highly doubtful, however, that many specimens are exported to meet the international demand for parrots. The race occupies an extremely restricted territory and, according to the limited data available, it is a race whose numbers are just as limited.

Yellow Naped Amazon, *A. o. auropalliata*. Sick birds such as this one should be isolated in their own cage so that they can receive extra warmth and special treatment.

AMAZONA OCHROCEPHALA AUROPALLIATA (LESSON)

"Its reputation as one of the best talking parrots is deserved." Paul Slud (1964).

A.o. auropalliata is more popularly known as the Yellow Naped Amazon or, more simply, the Yellow Nape.

Physical dimensions of A.o. auropalliata:

	Wing	Tail	Culmen	Tarsus
Males	215-234mm	106.5-125mm	34-37mm	25-29mm
Females	208-224mm	112.5-124mm	30.5-34.5mm	23.0-29mm

Physical Description

For some reason, the Yellow Nape Amazon is frequently confused with the Panama Amazon *(A.o. panamensis).* The reason for this confusion is not exactly clear; while the two subspecies have substantial differences in common as compared to the other subspecies of *A. ochrocephala,* there is an outstanding difference between the two: the Yellow Nape has a swath of yellow across the nape of its neck, whereas the Panama does not.

Furthermore, the Yellow Nape is more massive in appearance, and its head is distinctively larger. Finally, the Yellow Nape does not have the distinctive yellow coloring in the inner thighs which is common to the Panama.

HEAD: The majority of Yellow Napes have little or no yellow coloring to the head region, and this absence of coloration includes the lores, crown, cheeks, chin, occiput and hindneck. A few specimens, however, have a V-shaped band of yellow just above the beak; when there is such yellow coloration it is generally only a smattering, but in rare exceptions a specimen's coloration may extend to the forehead and even include the upper crown. In such deviations from the norm, however, the yellow never includes the lores or cheeks. While it may be possible to confuse such specimens with the Panama *(A.o. panamensis),* such Yellow Napes are still clearly distinguishable from Panamas because all Yellow Napes have a swath of yellow across their napes, a distinguishing characteristic not found in Panamas. Generally, this band is quite extensive. This yellow band is a subdued shade, and the band may vary in size from individual bird to individual bird.

103

The head feathers are slightly darker than the standard parrot green commonly found on most Amazons. The green, some feel, contains a hint of blue to it. Whatever the case, the Yellow Nape's green plumage is somewhat darker than that found on the Panama and decidedly darker than much of the yellowish green plumage found on most other subspecies of *A. ochrocephala*.

Both mandibles of the Yellow Nape's beak are charcoalish gray, gradually becoming bone-colored at the base of the upper mandible near the cere. The iris is a reddish burnt orange.

BODY: Both breast and back are slightly darker colored than the head region, giving an appearance of a somewhat solid and distinct parrot green. The breast coloration is a slightly lighter shade of green than the back.

WINGS: The bend of the wing is green, as is the carpal edge. The outer webs of the first four secondaries are poppy red, gradually phasing into yellow at the basal portion. The primaries are generally green at their proximal half but bluish black on the distal half, with the inner webs being somewhat slate gray. Both inner and outer web coverts are a yellowish green, with the inner coverts more lightly shaded than other feathers of the wing and considerably lighter in shade than upper wing coverts, which are more or less similar in hue to the rest of the green of the upper wing.

TAIL: While the basal portion of the tail's feathers is primarily parrot green, approximately half of the feathers' end color is a yellowish green. There is some red and yellow, however, on the inner webs of the outer five rectrices on both sides. Red generally predominates on the outer rectrices and yellow in the inner.

FEET: The thighs are green, similar to the other coloration of the lower torso. The legs and feet are dusty flesh colored.

IMMATURES: The only basic difference between mature and immature Yellow Napes is that immature specimens have no yellow on the forehead or nape-hindneck region. The nape hindneck region is a slightly lighter green color common to the remainder of the head. The iris is mahogany colored and the beak is entirely charcoalish gray. A bird eight to ten months old may still have no yellow on the nape, but usually a fleck or two of yellow may be seen at that age.

Geographical Distribution

While Salvin believed that "there is no authentic instance of this [i.e. *A.o. auropalliata*] parrot in Mexico" (Salvin, 1871) it is a well established species in the most southerly western Mexican states of Chiapas and Oaxaca, the latter forming the most northerly boundary of the Yellow Nape's range. Common to the Pacific Coast coastal plain in those two states, it ranges throughout most of Chiapas, which borders Guatemala, and follows the coastal plain through Guatemala, Honduras and El Salvador and then finally to northwestern Costa Rica, which forms the most southerly boundary of its range. This distance is approximately 1100 kilometers.

A.o. auropalliata appears to be more heavily concentrated along the Pacific coastal plains of Guatemala and northwestern Costa Rica, where it is reported by numerous observers as being common. In Guatemala it tends to prefer the dry forested regions on the Cordilleras' western side as opposed to the more open savanna type terrain of the coastal plain region. In the Cordilleras, it has been observed up to an altitude of 2000 feet above sea level, but it is infrequently seen in the central plateau.

While some mid-nineteenth century reports defined the subspecies's range as also including the eastern slopes of the Cordilleras and the Caribbean coastal regions of Guatemala and Honduras, it has long been accepted that the Yellow Nape's range is confined exclusively to the western side of the Cordilleras. Evidently the earlier view was based on a report by Franzius that he had observed the species in the wet forested regions at Sarapiqui on the eastern side of the Cordilleras in Costa Rica (Franzius, 1869). This view was eventually discarded; the current avigeographical position is that the race is confined to the Pacific slope of the Central American peninsula.

However, there may be sufficient reason to re-examine this view. In the year or so in which Slud lived in Costa Rica during the early 1960's, he did not see any wild specimens of *A.o. auropalliata* in the Sarapiqui lowlands, but he did report that "people native to the area spoke of a large green parrot with a yellow nape that could only be this species" (Slud, 1964). The possibility exists that *A.o. auropalliata* does exist, even while it

105

may be only in small, isolated flocks of limited populations, east of the Cordilleras. Monroe and Howell's 1966 field studies found similar populations of *A.o. parvipes* (the closest relative of *A.o. auropalliata*) in the Mosquitias region straddling the Honduran-Nicaraguan border along the Caribbean (Monroe and Howell, 1966). Additionally, it has long been recognized that a yellow-naped variety of *A. ochrocephala* was indigenous and common to Roatan Island, Honduras. The possibility does exist, however—and it should be noted—that if there are small scattered populations of *A.o. auropalliata* east of the Cordilleras they may be groups of escaped cage birds. San Jose, the capital of Costa Rica, situated east of the Cordilleras, has long been known to have *A. o. auropalliata* in its region, but the birds have been considered there only as escaped pets. However, given the frequency with which caged birds escape and the popularity of the Yellow Nape as a cage bird, there is no reason to reject the possibility that escaped birds can establish populations throughout the eastern Cordilleras, replenishing their numbers through breeding in a favorable and conducive environment.

Farther north, in the Honduran and Guatemalan regions, there has been speculation that the subspecies extends eastwards to the Atlantic so as to include the Sula Valley (Bailey and Conover, 1935) and perhaps even through the entire valley region to Roatan Island in Honduras. Such theories, however, were postulated on field studies prior to Monroe and Howell's field surveys along the Atlantic in the Mosquitias region, during which it was established that *A. o. parvipes* is the yellow-naped subspecies of *A. ochrocephala* in that area. *A.o. parvipes* was found to inhabit Roatan Island and the Mosquitias, and the possibility existed (based on two specimens collected in the Sula Valley) that the Atlantic coast portion of that valley was also part of that subspecies's normal range. The question, of course, is whether *A.o. parvipes* was isolated from the Pacific population or whether there is an integration line, however slim, between the ranges of *A.o. auropalliata* and *A.o. parvipes* somewhere in the Sula Valley region. This has not yet been determined.

Topographically, although Salvin maintained that *A.o. auropalliata* was common to the forest region (Salvin, 1871),

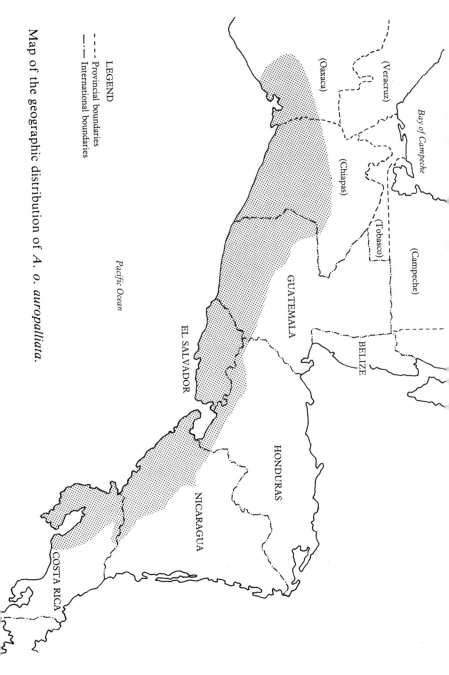

Map of the geographic distribution of *A. o. auropalliata.*

LEGEND
- - - - Provincial boundaries
- ·— International boundaries

Bay of Campeche

(Veracruz)

(Oaxaca)

(Chiapas)

(Tobasco)

(Campeche)

Pacific Ocean

GUATEMALA

BELIZE

EL SALVADOR

HONDURAS

NICARAGUA

COSTA RICA

subsequent field studies have shown this subspecies to prefer the semi-arid terrain common to savannas and dry woods (Davis, 1972). Slud (1964) noted that, additionally, the Yellow Nape could be frequently found in humid areas such as in the Gulf of Nicaragua. Yet while there is at least one report in addition to the one that identifies the Yellow Nape with wet forested areas, the accumulative evidence points out that the drier areas are preferred.

A. O. AUROPALLIATA AS A PET

The Yellow Naped Amazon is one of the most popular of all the subspecies of *A. ochrocephala*. It has always commanded a high premium; it is the highest-priced of all the subspecies. Indeed, at the time of this writing young birds are being offered for sale in the southern California area for $700. They are advertised as "beginning to talk" (*Los Angeles Times,* 1979).

The high premium placed on the Yellow Nape, aside from its desirability as a pet, is only in part caused by its general scarcity as contrasted to the relative abundance of the other subspecies, which can be found in quantity in pet shops after the end of the spring season. The bird's personality and performance are the deciding factors in pricing.

Most aviculturists and bird fanciers would categorize *A.o. auropalliata* as one of the top three or four best talkers of all parrot species and races recognized for their mimicry. Literature and legend could provide countless testimonials testifying to this bird's ability to talk. The experiences John Hettiger recollected about his pet Yellow Nape, Herman, are typical of Yellow Nape owners. Hettiger's Herman had a vocabulary of 52 words, some of them complete sentences (such as "Herman wants coffee") which he would repeat endlessly during the breakfast hour, until he was finally served coffee and toast. Herman was so proficient at learning, so intelligent and such an accomplished talker that "Things would only have to be said a couple of times and Herman would have it down pat, and would be repeating it over and over again so that I used Herman as an instructor in my bird training room to help teach the other birds . . ."(Hettiger, 1973).

The subspecies's desirable characteristics have been recognized for some time. For example, Underwood (1896) wrote of his

Sick Yellow Nape being spoon-fed.

observations of the Yellow Nape after extensive field studies in Central America: "The young are eagerly sought after, and the birds when they begin to talk, which is generally about a year old, sell for fairly good prices."

Besides its excellent talking ability, the Yellow Nape is easily acclimated to the human presence and reveals an amazing proclivity to tame rapidly. Better still, it accepts that kind of reciprocal relationship with its master which is essential if a parrot is to become a pet.

Bates and Busenbark, avid aviculturists and authors of several books on birds, made the following observation about the Yellow Nape: "For anyone wishing to have a parrot which is the most easily trained and a good performer, the writers unhesitatingly recommend a Yellow Naped Amazon" (Bates and Busenbark, 1978).

Perhaps the race's excellence as a pet parrot was best summarized by Dr. Greene, over a century ago:

> ... this is a very delightful species, clever, gentle, tractable, and less given to the undue exercise of its vocal abilities at their utmost pitch than many of its congeners; it is also handsome and hardy, and in a word, one to be highly recommended to the notice of amateurs.

A. o. auropalliata, the Yellow Naped Amazon. *A. o. parvipes,* a very rare form, is very hard to distinguish from *A. o. auropalliata.*

AMAZONA OCHROCEPHALA PARVIPES
(MONROE AND HOWELL)

Physical Dimensions of A.o. parvipes (Monroe and Howell, 1966):

	Wing	Tail	Culmen	Tarsus
Males	210-240.5mm	107-127.5mm	30.9-34mm	31.7-36.9mm
Females	204-228.5mm	102-113mm	30.3-34mm	29.5-34mm

Physical Description

A.o. parvipes proves to be one of the rarer subspecies of the *A. ochrocephala* complex; indeed, it was not classified until 1966. In personal communication with Dr. Thomas R. Howell at the University of California, Los Angeles, I was informed that *A.o. parvipes* is identical in appearance to *A.o. auropalliata*, except for the following differences: *A.o. parvipes* is a somewhat smaller bird, the difference being statistically significant; the bill is less pigmented, the bend of the wing has less red, and the feet are smaller. As far as Dr. Howell was aware, there were currently no photographs of this bird in the United States.

Note: The Monroe and Howell statistical analysis of size differences and the consequential significance must be viewed carefully, for the analysis was conducted with well below the minimum number of samples required for reasonable assurance that the results are reliable.

Geographical Distribution

Although *A.o. parvipes* was classified as a subspecies in 1966, as a member of the *A. ochrocephala* complex it had already been observed and identified in the Islas de la Bahias region of Honduras over a century ago.

By the 1800's specimens had been collected and the bird classified as *A.o. auropalliata*, the Yellow Naped Amazon. Reclassification was to follow only after an intervening period lasting almost one hundred years. In the meantime, *A.o. auropalliata* was described in much of the literature as having a range which included *only* the Pacific side of the Central

American peninsula, with the one Caribbean coast area exception being Roatan Island in the Islas de la Bahia.

As is true in so many cases where there is some variation in a given population, the question can be raised about whether or not *A. o. parvipes* is a distinct subspecies. The statistical analysis has been based on insufficient numbers of specimens. In the meantime, however, *A. o. parvipes* provides an interesting history illustrating the kinds of methodological problems encountered by ornithology when dealing with geographic isolation of groups of birds and classification systems.

While there have been some studies in the Honduran and eastern Nicaraguan areas, such studies are few and far between, with most ornithological interest devoted to other regions of the Central American peninsula—this despite the fact that there is an extensive and dramatic avifauna to study in the former regions. This absence of detailed field studies has resulted in significant gaps in fully understanding the complete geographical distribution of *A. ochrocephala* in Central America and *A.o. auropalliata* and/or *A.o. parvipes* in particular.

A.o. parvipes also probably escaped attention because it is limited to extremely small geographical areas: Roatan Island and some of the smaller islands in the immediate vicinity (twenty to thirty square kilometers) of the Islas de la Bahia group, the immediate Caribbean border area between Nicaragua and Honduras (approximately 7000 square kilometers), and a possible third location in the Sula Valley (about another 5000-6000 square kilometers). Additionally, given the sightings made by Monroe and Howell, it appears that *A.o. parvipes* is uncommon, particularly on the mainland, except in the Mosquitias Region. Finally, since *A.o. parvipes* was not observed between the eastern regions where it was collected and the Sula Valley district in the west, there is a strong possibility that there is no continuity of population along the Caribbean coast linking the two areas. If there *is* a population, it is probably rare in the intermediate zone, if indeed the two specimens collected in the east are representative of a native population there.

Another difficulty in establishing the complete geographic extent of the subspecies is that two color group types are found in the Sula Valley, but while there are reports of large flocks of yellow-crowned birds, there have been no reports of yellow-naped variations except for two collected specimens. It is not clear whether these two specimens are escaped pet birds or whether they are native to the area.

Historically, prior to 1860 it was generally believed that *Amazona ochrocephala* was confined solely to the western coast of Guatemala (Sclater and Salvin, 1859). In 1860, however, Cavendish Taylor was to travel across Honduras from west to east. After studying the avifauna on Islas Tigre in the Golfo de Fonesca in Honduras, he found *A.o. auropalliata* common on the island; he did not notice another specimen of *Amazona ochrocephala* until he reached Lake Yohoa, on the eastern side of the Cordilleras, a distance of approximately 150 kilometers, where he observed ". . .there is a parrot much resembling this [i.e., the *A.o. auropalliata* of Tigre Island] in plumage, but rather smaller, with the yellow on the forepart of the head instead of behind" (Taylor, 1860).

There was no further mention of *Amazona ochrocephala* in the region again until 1887 and then again in 1889, when two separated and isolated collections had been made, the collections in two of the three areas currently defined by Monroe and Howell as common to *A.o. parvipes:* the Islas de la Bahia on the northern coast of Honduras and the Mosquitias region sprawling across the international boundary between Honduras and Nicaragua in the east.

In 1887 a certain Charles Townsend had been collecting in the Mosquitias area, an arid lowland region. Details of the Townsend field expedition were published in a paper by Ridgway in which he identified the *A. ochrocephala* individual collected by Townsend, which had been localized by the collector as *Segovia R., Honduras,* as *A.o. auropalliata* (Ridgway, 1887).

In 1889, Salvin reported details on a collection made by Gaumer on Roatan Island, the largest island of the Islas de la Bahia group, in which five specimens of *A.o. auropalliata* had been collected. Salvin was to write of those specimens that it was ". . . the first we have received from any place on the eastern side of the Central American Cordillera" (Salvin, 1889).

Both the Townsend- and Gaumer-collected specimens in fact extended the range of *A.o. auropalliata* across the Peninsula from coast to coast. What was not clear was whether the race extended its range as a continuity across and over the Cordilleras, through the Sula Valley and hence to the Caribbean, or whether the Atlantic coast *A.o. auropalliata* was in fact an isolated population. If it was an isolated population, the possibility existed that it might be a distinct and separate variation of *Amazona ochrocephala*. This possibility was not considered, however, until the Monroe and Howell studies during the 1960's.

For almost thirty years the region remained absent from ornithological interest, at least as far as parrot studies were concerned, until 1916 when Ridgway wrote his comprehensive *The Birds of North and Middle America*, a complete compilation of all data gathered to date on all species identified in North America, in which he classified an *A. ochrocephala* collected by an E. Wittkugel as an *A.o. auropalliata*. This individual bird had been collected at Chasignua in the area of La Lima, Honduras (Ridgway, 1916).

La Lima is located in the upper Sula Valley region, an area also populated with a yellow-crowned type *A. ochrocephala,* a type not yet identified or classified by race. The Wittkugel specimen, collected in 1892, was the first of the two yellow naped types to be collected in the Sula Valley region. The skin of the Wittkugel specimen is housed at the Carnegie Museum and was examined by Dr. Monroe.

In 1929 Bangs collected a second specimen near La Lima (Peters, 1929), within fifty kilometers of the Wittkugel specimen. No further specimens have been seen or captured in the area. While the upper Sula Valley has been identified as one of the three areas of inhabitation for the race, Monroe (1968) has noted with reservation that the two specimens ". . . may possibly be vagrants or escaped cage birds."

Shortly after, in 1930, a specimen which was subsequently identified by Stone as *A.o. auropalliata* was collected near the coast in northeastern Honduras at Laguna Toloa by Emlen and Worth (Stone, 1932). Until that specimen was once again re-examined approximately thirty-five years later by Monroe and Howell, who found it to be not an *A.o. auropalliata* but a yellow-crowned type

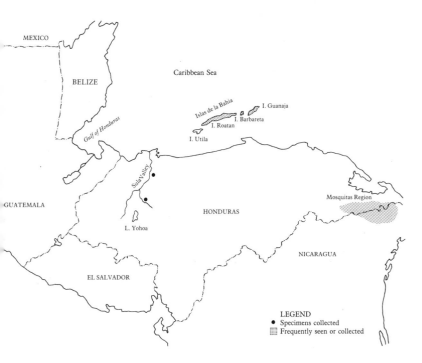

Map of the geographic distribution of *A. o. parvipes.*

of *A. ochrocephala,* the presence of the yellow-naped type in the Sula Valley was more or less established. It may have been Stone's identification of the Emlen and Worth specimen which prompted Peters in his *Check-List of Birds of the World* (1937) to define the range of *A.o. auropalliata* ". . .into the Caribbean lowlands of northern Honduras east to the Ulua Valley; Roatan Island." Given the Monroe and Howell examination of the specimen in question, however, the reliability of the Sula Valley region as being relevant to *A.o. parvipes* is less certain.

With the Islas de la Bahia and the Mosquitias region there is no question that there are viable populations of the yellow-naped variety in both localities. In addition to the individuals collected on Roatan by Gaumer last century, Bond reported the species common on Isla Guanaja east of Roatan after a field study there in

1936 (Bond, 1936). Monroe reports that Arthur Twomey and Roland Hawkins subsequently not only found the subspecies common on Guanaja but also on the islet of Barbareta, approximately three kilometers from the most eastern tip of Roatan (Monroe and Howell, 1966), but it is not reported from Utila Island, the remaining island of the Islas de la Bahia group and the one closest to the mainland.

While specimens of *A.o. auropalliata* were observed by Howell in the Mosquitias area in 1955, there was no effort to collect specimens until 1962 and 1963. In 1964 Monroe found the bird common in the Puerto Lempira area of the Laguna de Caratasca near the Segovia River, which forms part of the boundary between Nicaragua and Honduras. In the meantime, Howell was able to collect several specimens from the Mosquitias area in Nicaragua (Monroe and Howell, 1966).

Close study of the specimens observed and collected from the Islas de la Bahias population and the Mosquitias region with the two specimens collected in the Sula Valley region, prove them to share the same physical characteristics differentiating them from *A.o. auropalliata*. Statistical analyses of the size differentials between the Pacific and Atlantic coast specimens of *A.o. auropalliata* were found to be significant, and the Caribbean population was reclassified as *Amazona ochrocephala parvipes*. It should also be noted that besides the size differential, there are color differences.

Several questions still remain to be resolved, however. It is still not certain whether the Sula Valley specimens represent anything more than escaped cage birds. If, however, *A.o. parvipes* is indigenous to the area, it then still remains to be ascertained whether it intergrades at some western point in the Sula Valley or the Cordilleras with *A. o. auropalliata*. Judging from the present evidence, it would appear that *A.o. auropalliata* does not extend its range eastwards beyond the western slopes of the Cordilleras.

Finally, while *A.o. parvipes* stretches across the Nicaraguan-Honduran border in the Mosquitias region, it is still not clear what the most southerly extent of its range is in Nicaragua. Also, we do not know whether there is a continuity of population between Honduras's eastern extremes and the western regions adjacent to and including the Sula Valley.

Young parrots—an Amazon, a macaw and a female Eclectus. It will be several years before any of these birds are mature and ready to breed.

A. O. PARVIPES AS A PET

We do not know anything definite about *A.o. parvipes* as a cage bird. It could be assumed, however, that given the minor differences between *A.o. auropalliata* and *A.o. parvipes*, there is probably not too much difference in disposition and ability to talk between the two races. Given the Yellow Nape's gentle disposition and propensity to mimic with excellence, there is probably every reason to believe that *A.o. parvipes* will prove just as excellent a cage bird as the Yellow Nape.

Given its rarity, it is doubtful that many *A.o. parvipes* individuals ever find their way into the United States or other foreign pet markets.

Yellow Naped Amazon, *A. o. auropalliata*. In the past, when the forms of *A. ochrocephala* were less well known, *A. o. auropalliata* was sometimes referred to as the "Panama Parrot," or even the "Panama Amazon."

AMAZONA OCHROCEPHALA PANAMENSIS (CABANIS)

A.o. panamensis is popularly called the Panama Amazon.

Physical dimensions of A.o. panamensis

	Wing	Tail	Culmen	Tarsus
Males	191-213mm	94-112mm	29-32mm	23-25mm
Females	190-212mm	92-109mm	28.5-33mm	23-26mm

Physical Description

The Panama Amazon is sometimes confused with the Yellow Naped Amazon *(A.o. auropalliata)* and sometimes, while not as frequently, with the Single Yellow Head *(A.o. ochrocephala)*. For a complete discussion of the salient differences between the Panama and these subspecies, see the other sections.

HEAD: The Panama has, more or less, a restricted swath of yellow stretching from the cere to the forehead, and at times the yellow may extend to the anterior portion of the crown. This yellow coloration may also extend downwards to include the lores. Frequently the yellow may be found to be suffused with green; in some specimens there may be almost no yellow whatever on the forehead crown region. Some specimens have a tinge of red to the basal part of their forehead yellow feathers.

The areas immediately bordering the yellow swath on the upper parts of the head are a bluish green, but the remainder of the head phases into a more distinctly yellowish green.

The periophthalmic region is less pronounced than usual and is a somewhat tannish color. The iris is a burnt orange. The lower mandible is slate gray, and while the lower half of the upper mandible is also similarly colored, the upper portion adjacent to and including the cere is a dark tan color.

BODY: The body, including both back and breast, is a generally uniform parrot green, with the breast feathers containing a hint of yellow.

WINGS: The bend of the wing is poppy red, but the amount of coverage varies from individual to individual so that on some specimens the red is visible only when the wing is extended. The

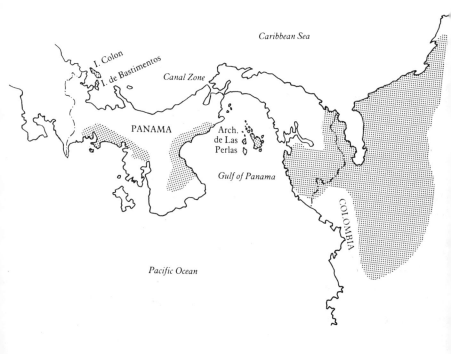

Map of the geographic distribution of *A. o. panamensis.*

carpal edge is generally a light yellowish green which may or may not contain some flecks of red to it.

The upper coverts are a parrot green edged along the distal edges with a yellowish green. The distal half of the primaries is a violet blue coloration, with the inner webs tending towards a slate black shade while the remainder is a typical parrot-green coloration. The first four secondaries have poppy red outerwebs tipped in a violet blue. The basal portion, like the primaries, is a parrot green.

The under coverts are a distinct green, almost yellow green.

TAIL: For approximately halfway from the basal part of the four outer tail feathers on each side to the immediate area, the color is basically green, with the extreme basal portion of both webs a

120

light poppy red color. The distal portion is a lighter shade of green, a yellowish green. The upper and lower tail coverts are a lighter yellowish green than the surrounding plumage.

FEET: Both inner and outer thighs are a yellowish green. Depending on the individual bird, some specimens may have a greater degree of yellowish green on the inner thighs or various degrees of yellow suffused throughout the inner thigh plumage.

The feet are a grayish tan color; the claws are ebony black.

IMMATURES: The immature *A.o. panamensis* has a brownish black iris and less red on the tail or bend of the wing, and the thighs may be a distinct green color. The forehead is usually green.

For the most part it would be accurate to say that an immature *A.o. panamensis* is basically a green parrot, although birds which are 8 or 9 months old may have some limited yellow to the forehead. Younger birds recently from the nest have dark brown/black eyes.

Note: A.o. panamensis is generally somewhat smaller than the Yellow Naped Amazon *(A.o. auropalliata)* and the Single Yellow Head *(A.o. ochrocephala)*, the two subspecies with which it is sometimes confused. Additionally, *A.o. panamensis* has a somewhat shorter and squatter tail.

Geographical Distribution

The Panama's range includes the tropical zones of Panama and a significant portion of the northern and central regions of Colombia.

In Panama, the race is confined primarily to the Pacific Coast region, where it is found as far west as Chiriqui (Bangs, 1901). Its Pacific Coast range extends eastwards along the peninsula to include the drier and eastern section of the Azuero Peninsula, where the subspecies was described by Wetmore (1968) as being common. Farther east, in the Gulf of Panama region, they have been observed as common on the Archipelago Perlas in the past, and more recently, Wetmore (1968) observed them flying between the islands and the open stretches of water to the mainland. They are now considered to be rare in the Panama Canal Zone (Eisenman and Loftin, 1968).

Taming and training a Yellow Fronted Amazon while it is still young will help to lessen the unpredictability of these birds.

The subspecies is not a common resident on the Caribbean coast region of Panama. There are two territorial exceptions, however: Wetmore (1968) did see a pair of Panamas at Bocas del Toro on the island of Colon in the western region of the country near Costa Rica and at Puerto Obaldia next to the Panama-Colombia border. It has not been determined whether the populations in these two areas are common or not.

A.o. panamensis is considered to extend its range throughout the entire tropical zone of central and northern Colombia (Meyer de Schauensee, 1964). Dugand (1947) considered it the most common of the Amazon group in the northern Colombian area consisting of the regions near Fundacion and Santa Marta.

The Colombian range of the Panama is considered at present to include the territory east of the Andes in the tropical zone (Chapman, 1928), as far east as the area around and including Bogota, particularly in the Magdelena Valley area (Chapman, 1928), as far south along the western extremes of its range at Hondo, and throughout the northern provinces adjacent to the mouth of the Magdalena River. It can be described as common throughout its Colombian range.

A. O. PANAMENSIS AS A PET

Of all the diverse subspecies of *A. ochrocephala*, the Panama is one of the most desirable of all. It is the rare Panama which does not prove to be an exceptional pet and unexcelled talker. Frequently, if acquired young enough so that they must still be hand-fed until they are capable of feeding themselves, such young birds will have acquired a small vocabulary by the time they are five or six months old.

Succinctly, there is no praise which can be considered an over-exaggeration in describing the Panama Amazon. The behavior of almost every pet Panama is the embodiment of what most parrot fanciers would hope to achieve in a parrot. In addition, it is a hardy pet.

Because it is such an outstanding parrot, the Panama often is more expensive than most other subspecies of *A. ochrocephala*. The best time to purchase a Panama Amazon is during February and March, when supplies of baby birds are still available.

Single Yellow Head, *A. o. ochrocephala*. The Single Yellow Head is probably the most widely kept of all the *A. ochrocephala* subspecies. It is popular as a caged bird both in the United States and in South America, and while some unfairly describe it as a poor talker, its talking performance belies that myth. Because of its easy accessibility, its pleasant disposition and its low cost compared to the other subspecies, it is highly recommended as a pet.

AMAZONA OCHROCEPHALA
OCHROCEPHALA (GMELIN)

A.o. ochrocephala enjoys a number of popular names: Single Yellow Head, Yellow Head, Yellow Fronted Amazon, Colombian Parrot and, in Spanish speaking countries, Loro Real.

Physical dimensions of A. o. ochrocephala:

	Wings	**Tail**	**Culmen**	**Tarsus**
Males	200-222mm	106-125mm	31-36mm	25-27.5mm
Females	201-220mm	107-124mm	29-33mm	25-27mm

Physical Description

A.o. ochrocephala is sometimes confused with the Panama Amazon *(A.o. panamensis)*, a parrot with some general similarities. There is a considerable difference between the two subspecies, however, and a simple observation of the basic differences should eliminate confusion. There are certain specific differences to note.

A.o. ochrocephala has more extensive yellow coverage to the head, the yellow beginning at the forehead and extending to the crown, often as far back as the occiput. This yellow is a bright coloration, clearly delineated and rarely suffused with green, unlike what is often the case with the Panama. The Panama has far less yellow; the band is not as wide and does not extend to the rear of the crown; additionally, the yellow is frequently contaminated with green.

A second basic difference between the two subspecies is in the coloration of the beak: the Panama's beak is a slate black coloration from cere to tip, whereas the Yellow Head's is horn colored with a dark brown tip. Additionally, the periophthalmic region of the Yellow Head is distinctly white, making the eye stand out, whereas the Panama has a periophthalmic region which is more dull gray than white. The Panama's ring is less extensive in size and less prominent, almost to the extent of being non-existent as a distinct color deviation from the surrounding plumage coloration.

HEAD: As noted above, the distinctly bright yellow swath on the head begins at the cere to include the forehead, crown and sometimes the forefront of the occiput. This coverage is confined to solely the top of the head and does not extend downwards to in-

125

clude the lores and cheeks or ear coverts. The band of yellow is clearly delineated and is separated from the periophthalmic region by the marked band of green which proceeds around the eye area to cover the remainder of the head in the same color.

This green coverage is a uniformly bright dark green which differs very little in tone or tint from the green shade common to the rest of the body, including the breast. The bill is horn colored and somewhat glossy. The lower third of the upper mandible is a dark brown/slate color. The immediate area surrounding each nostril is similarly colored. The periophthalmic region is a white skin which stands out sharply and clearly. The iris is a burnt orange color.

BODY: The back feathers of *A.o. ochrocephala* are uniformly a bright dark green. The breast is a slightly lighter shade of the same coloration, but under strong lighting the breast feathers seem to have a tinge of yellow in them. As with the back feathers, there is no variation in shade from one region of the body to another, except for the vent region where the immediate feathers are a distinctly yellow-shaded green.

WINGS: The bend of the wing is red, but the coverage of red coloration is so limited that usually, unless the wing is spread out, there is no indication of color. Sometimes, more or less yellow may suffuse the red in the bend. The carpal edge is green.

As with other subspecies of *A. ochrocephala*, the primaries are green at their basal portion and a violet blue at their distal region. The outer four secondaries are poppy red distally and a yellowish green at the basal section.

The under coverts are yellowish green, but the over coverts resemble the back feathers in shade of coloration.

TAIL: The basal part of the outer tail feathers is red. The intermediate portions of the tail are green but with a broad terminal band of yellowish green at the distal portion.

FEET: Both inner and outer thighs are similarly toned in a shade identical to the breast region, but the inner thighs may sometimes have flecks of yellow interspersed in lower regions.

The feet are a dark horn gray color.

Immatures: The immature *A. o. ochrocephala* can easily be mistaken for the young of other *Amazona* species. The extremely young will have little or no red to the bend of the wing. Until approximately seven months old, their eyes are a dark brown-black. There may be little or no yellow to the forehead.

Geographical Distribution

The Single Yellow Head enjoys an extensive geographical range, being perhaps the only other subspecies of *A. ochrocephala* to rival the extensive range of *A.o. oratrix*. Initially, the race was considered to have a limited range in Venezuela only (Berlepsch, 1902), but subsequent field studies have found that the range extends into several countries of northern South America.

The subspecies's range extends eastwards as far as Guyana, and while it is rare along the coastal regions (McLoughlin, 1970), it is more commonly found in the interior. Bangs and Penard (1918) did not find it in Surinam, however, which makes Guyana its most easterly boundary. Its most southeasterly reaches are in the Rio Branco region of northern Brazil, an area in the vicinity where the Guyana, Venezuelan and Brazilian borders intersect. Its range extends westwards through the Amazon, but Pinto (1966) found that the subspecies does not appear to extend its range below the lower reaches of the Amazon River.

In the west, its boundaries stretch to the eastern Andes Mountains (Chapman, 1917) in Peru and Colombia. The species was found to be equally at home in both primal forest and coffee plantation. In the north, in Venezuela, it is common to both tropical forests and the coastal plains (Schafer and Phelps, 1958) .

A. O. OCHROCEPHALA AS A PET

The Single Yellow Head is, unfortunately, not given the credit that it truly deserves. More often than not, *A.o. ochrocephala* is judged solely on its speaking ability; depending on the authority evaluating the subspecies, it is rated anywhere from "as a talking pet, it is excellent" (Bates and Busenbark, 1978) to "it is not a spectacular talker" (Freud, 1974). Usually, most opinions agree with the latter opinion, and *A.o. ochrocephala* is frequently passed over for other parrots or parrot types.

Like all other subspecies of *A. ochrocephala*, the Single Yellow

Map of the geographic distribution of *A. o. ochrocephala.*

Head proves to be a superior talker compared to the multitude of other species and subspecies available to bird fanciers. Additionally, the Single Yellow Head proves to have a colorful personality and the propensity to become an affectionate pet—if given the opportunity.

While *A.o. ochrocephala* is not an extremely popular subspecies in the United States, it is nevertheless accorded an excellent reputation in South America. For example, as early as 1913, while on a field expedition into the Orinoco region of northern South America, Cherrie reported that *A.o. ochrocephala* is "... most sought after as a pet (although almost never caged) by the natives, and there is scarcely a house in the country districts where one or more is not to be seen" (Cherrie, 1916).

This opinion of the Orinoco residents can have value only when it is considered that the Single Yellow Head is only one of a total of 29 different species of parrots and parrot types which can easily be caught in the region—and this does not include a diversity of subspecies!

In the United States, *A.o. ochrocephala* is reasonably available most of the year; yet while the subspecies is not viewed favorably by some, it still proves to be a perennially good-selling race. People who have purchased one as a pet are rarely disappointed. *A.o. ochrocephala* elicits praise from its North American owners as well as South Americans. For example, John Hettiger, an aviculturist and bird fancier for years, one who has been so active with parrots that he has been training as many as twenty at one time, wrote a delightful article in *American Cage-Bird Magazine*, "The Most Unforgettable Parrots in My Life," in which he reminisces over some of the birds he has owned and trained. He writes: "I could talk to you about many birds, but the parrot that stands out at the top of the list is 'Pretty Boy,' a Single Yellow Head." Pretty Boy, while admittedly having a limited vocabulary, enjoyed riding on the handlebars of Hettiger's son's bike; while riding he would laugh at passing cars and would call out 'hello' to children. He apparently enjoyed having a bath with the same lad, and with just as much relish enjoyed 'running and splashing' through mud puddles after a rain (Hettiger, 1973). Undoubtedly, given the space, Hettiger could have filled an entire magazine with similar stories in detail.

Hettiger's Pretty Boy is not an exceptional *A.o. ochrocephala*. The Single Yellow Head will prove itself almost every time if given the opportunity to develop a trust in people. Unfortunately, many pet owners give up too soon, forgetting that the Single Yellow Head tends to be a timid fellow. Friends of the writer, Keith and Margie Pendell of La Habra, California, have a Single Yellow Head called Pedro who took almost four months before he could feel comfortable with people. In addition to his timidity, which he has basically overcome by now, he has proved himself to have an excellent memory. Three months after I 'worked' Pedro to show Keith how to train the bird, Pedro still remembers me and resorts to a regression in which he makes baby sounds of fear

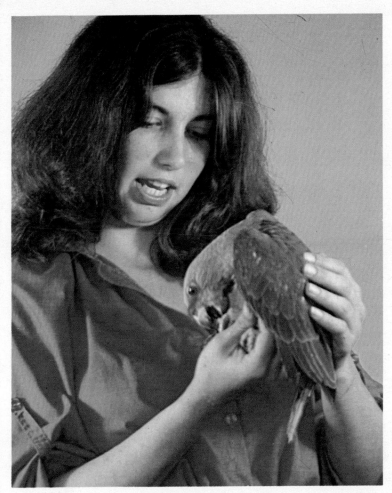

This young Yellow Nape, held by Laura Hill, is approximately eight months old. This youngster was wild prior to the photography session, but after about five minutes of handling, the bird could be trusted to sit on her arm without biting.

Opposite:
Yellow Naped Amazon, *A. o. auropalliata*.
Many knowledgeable bird fanciers believe the
Yellow Nape has the best disposition of all of
the *A. ochrocephala* subspecies.

Single Yellow Head, *A. o. ochrocephala*. In those regions where the Single Yellow Head is common, it is considered the best talker of all species of Amazons.

every time the author is in his presence. While he has not forgiven me, he has become a charming and delightful pet for the Pendells.

This timidity, which reflects itself in a very great fear of being touched by the hand, is common to adult birds when first acquired, even after the bird has been tamed. It is only after a degree of trust has been developed that this timidity is discarded. As an excellent illustration, Freud wrote about his pet, Valentine, who was so timid that not only would he push the hand away with his foot if someone attempted to pick him up, but he refused to eat when his food was placed before him so long as a person was in the room. Freud was pleased to report that Valentine overcame his fears (as is the experience of most other owners of this subspecies) and has not only learned to play a variety of games with his owner but also enjoys nibbling on the owner's hand and ring (Freud, 1974).

Because of the Single Yellow Head's timidity, it is best to purchase specimens as pets when they are under a year of age. The younger, of course, the better. Older birds may be just too old to learn to trust humans.

The Single Yellow Head has one final advantage at present over other subspecies of *A. ochrocephala*: this subspecies has provided ornithology and aviculture most of their data on breeding behavior. This subspecies has shown a willingness to breed in captivity. It makes an excellent parrot for the advanced aviculturist interested in breeding Amazon parrots. It should be remembered, however, that birds that have been tamed and transformed into pets tend to lose most of their instinctual drives.

A plan to breed *A.o. ochrocephala*, therefore, should be treated as a long-term project, because the birds should be young when acquired: they do not reach breeding age until their fifth or sixth year. Finally, because *A. ochrocephala* is not sexually dimorphic, additional birds may be required should the original pair prove to be of the same sex.

Above and opposite: Yellow Naped Amazon, *A. o. auropalliata*. Note the differences in coloration with increasing maturity. The photo above shows a youngster less than one year old, without any yellow coloration whatsoever to forehead or nape. The top photo on the opposite page shows a young adult approximately three years old. The nape of this specimen still shows some green. Additionally, it has not yet acquired any yellow on the forehead. The bottom photo on the opposite page shows a fully mature adult.

This is a good illustration of the kind of response a tame Yellow Nape, *A. o. auropalliata,* can produce.

AMAZONA OCHROCEPHALA NATTERERI (FINSCH)

A.o. nattereri is most generally known as Natterer's Amazon.
Physical dimensions of A. o. nattereri:

	Wing	Tail	Culmen	Tarsus
Male	218-238mm	119-126mm	31-35mm	26.5-28.5mm
Female	210-231mm	107-125mm	30-36mm	26-29mm

Note: The female is usually smaller than the male. However, as is also true of all other *A. ochrocephala* subspecies, there are many females larger than males. Size cannot be used as an accurate measure of sex differentiation. There are no dimorphic features.

Physical Description

Natterer's Amazon is not commonly imported into the United States or Europe. Actually, it could be described as a rare cage bird in both places. It is sometimes confused with *Amazona farinosa guatemalae* (Hellmayr, 1910), but there should be no reason for confusion—*A.o. nattereri* has red to the bend of the wing, whereas *A.f. guatemalae* does not. Apart from *A.o. xantholaema* (whose status is in doubt) Natterer's Amazon is the only subspecies of *A. ochrocephala* that has a blue cast to its head coloration.

A.o. nattereri is primarily like *A.o. ochrocephala* in appearance except for the blue tinge to the green head plumage and its size, which is somewhat larger than the Single Yellow Head.

HEAD: As with *A.o. ochrocephala*, Natterer's Amazon has a broad frontal band of yellow stretching from the forehead to crown, with no yellow on the side of the head whatever. Unlike *A.o. ochrocephala*, however, the region between the yellow on the forehead-crown swath and the eyes is a distinct blue-green on Natterer's as opposed to the green of the Single Yellow Head. This blue green tints all plumage on the cheeks, ear coverts and upper throat regions.

The iris is orange-yellow. The beak is horn-colored, with the tip of the upper mandible a brownish gray.

BODY: While the dorsal side is a uniformly bright dark green, the breast area may have a blue tint to the green.

WINGS: As with all other subspecies of *A. ochrocephala*, Natterer's Amazon has red to the bend of the wing. The carpal edge is

The Mexican Double Yellow Head, *A. o. oratrix,* is by far the most commonly recognized, owned and desired parrot of the *ochrocephala* subspecies. Also known simply as the Double Yellow Head, it is a versatile and fluent talker, although its disposition can sometimes not be trusted. Young birds, such as this particular specimen, can be hand-trained within a few minutes. Prior to the photography session, Casey Ross worked with this bird for approximately ten minutes. Although still basically wild, it remained calm throughout the session.

The Double Yellow Head occurs in Mexico only. These two fine young birds are less than eight months old. The specimen to the left is already beginning to show the promise of the yellow head coverage for which this subspecies is noted.

also red. Again as with all other *A. ochrocephala* subspecies, the speculum of the wing is a bright poppy red, with the basal portions of the four secondaries a yellowish green. The under coverts are a darker shaded yellowish green. The primaries are the same as in the other subspecies, blue-black at the distal portions of the inner webs and violet blue on outer webs.

TAIL: The tail is a parrot green except for the two inner feathers, which are a yellowish green. The under tail coverts are a faint yellow green.

FEET: The inner and outer thighs are alike in coloration. The feet are a brownish gray color.

IMMATURES: Until about seven months of age, the eyes are a dark slate grayish brown. There is less coloration on the forehead crown region, with the yellow being more or less confined to the forehead. There is little or no red to the carpal edge or bend of the wing.

Geographical Distribution

A.o. nattereri is confined primarily to the central region of South America in a range stretching from the east to the northwest. Its territorial range remains well south of the Amazon River and approaches the range of *A.o. ochrocephala* only in the northern part of the continent at the province of Caqueta in southern Colombia, where the two subspecies are separated by only about 100 kilometers (Dugand and Borrero, 1948).

Its most easterly range in Brazil is at Labaryi in the Rio de Janeiro region; this is more or less its most southerly range near the Atlantic Coast. The race is common to Matto Grosso province, (Ihering, 1907), stretching its range northwestwards to the foothills of the Andes in the Rio Maranon region of eastern Peru (Naumberg, 1930). The western extent of the range follows northwards along the foothills of the Andes through Ecuador, its most western boundaries appearing to be Sarayacu and as far north as Florencia in southern Colombia.

While the range of *A.o. nattereri* on the western side of the continent stretches into its northern reaches, in Brazil the race is primarily restricted to the southern part of the country which forms the greater extent of the race's territory.

Map of the geographic distribution of *A. o. nattereri.*

A. O. NATTERERI AS A PET

Natterer's Amazon is infrequently found in the United States as a caged pet bird. I have not yet had the opportunity to see a live one, and despite the extensive library research conducted to provide historical material for this book, there was not one article which could shed any light on the bird's behavior in captivity. As a matter of fact, every standard book on parrots used by bird fanciers and aviculturists either says nothing about the behavior of this subspecies or totally excludes it from the contents.

This is another still immature Double Yellow Head, *A. o. oratrix*. Note, however, that while this specimen is only two-and-a-half to three years old, the yellow is already beginning to show the extent to which it will color the entire head and neck region. Compare the amount of yellow on this specimen's "booties" (the feathers in the lower thigh region) with that of the two specimens in the preceding photograph.

Yellow Fronted Amazons, like many other psittacine species, can be trained to perform various tricks. This Double Yellow Head, *A. o. oratrix,* approximately three years old, will lie on its back without much coaxing. Part of the Schuelke collection, it is one of their many parrots which have been taught a variety of tricks.

A.O. XANTHOLAEMA (BERLEPSCH)

This subspecies was first classified by Count von Berlepsch in 1913; he reported on two specimens collected on Marajo Island situated at the mouth of the Amazon River in Brazil. There have been no further specimens collected or reported since then. Since there are only two specimens known, there is sufficient reason to question the validity of the classification until, at least, other specimens can be collected from the same region. While most ornithological check lists include *A.o. xantholaema* as a subspecies, there are few authors who do not raise the issue of the bird's classification. Rather than attempt to describe *xantholaema* or make any observations apart from those noted above, it might be best simply to quote the original publication of the bird's discovery verbatim. There is nothing more than can be added to the original account, which appeared in *Ornithologische Monats Berichte;* a translation follows:

> Description of Two New Bird Species which were discovered by Dr. Bluntschli and Dr. Peyer on the Island of Marajo in the Delta of the Amazon River.
> by Count von Berlepsch

Amazons which are very tame—like this Yellow Nape—often enjoy having their heads scratched.

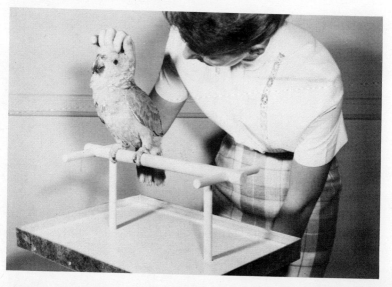

Because this Yellow Nape's wings have been clipped, the bird cannot fly from the parrot stand.

Amazona ochrocephala xantholaema
Description of specimen in the Senckenberg Collection ("Marajo near the hacienda St. Andre, June 3, 1910. Iris orange, orange spots on sides of bases of upper part of bill." Bluntschli and Peyer)

The only existing specimen, an undoubtedly mature bird, is so dramatically different from other specimens in the Berlepsch Collection from the central and lower Orinoco Region [an area near the Venezuelan-Brazilian border in the north central region of Brazil] that it must be regarded as a new kind, which is, nevertheless, similar to *Amazona ochrocephala*.

The bird from Marajo is not only larger with a stronger and longer bill, but also different in coloration. The sides of the head are not green like all other specimens of *Amazona ochrocephala* that I have examined, but vividly yellow [that is, in comparison with *A.o. ochrocephala*]. The yellow coloration on the top of the head extends much farther over the back of the head. The narrow band of color on the forehead is iridescent green instead of yellowish green. The tibias are colored yellow instead of green.

Chico is a Double Yellow Head, *A. o. oratrix,* approximately three years old. One of the fine birds of the Schuelke collection, Chico shows a distinct preference for his mistress, Tracy Schuelke, and allows her to handle him in ways not permitted others. While Double Yellow Heads have a reputation for being somewhat unpredictable, this fine bird has a cheerful and pleasant disposition.

Of these young Amazons, the Double Yellow Head, *A. o. oratrix* (near the gray cup), is approximately one year older than the Tres Marias, *A. o. tresmariae* (near the light green cup). Note that the yellow coloration of the throat of *oratrix* is complete, even though the yellow of the back of the head and the cheek regions has yet to appear. The *tresmariae* is already beginning to grow yellow feathers in the back of the head. The chief difference between these two birds, however, is in the *hue* of yellow. Note that the *tresmariae's* yellow is a lighter and somewhat brighter shade than that of the *oratrix.*

147

Bibliography

Bailey, Alfred M. and H.B. Conover. "Notes from the State of Durango, Mexico." *Auk,* Vol. II, 1935, pp. 421-471.

Bailey, H.H. "Ornithological Notes from Western Mexico and Tres Marias and Isabella Islands." *Auk,* Vol. 28, 1906, pp. 369-391.

Bangs, O. "On a Collection of Birds made by W.W. Brown, Jr. at David and Divala, Chiriqui." *Auk,* Vol. 18, 1901, pp. 355-370.

Bangs, O. and J. Penard. "Notes on a Collection of Surinam Birds." *Bulletin of the Museum of Comparative Zoology,* LXII, #2, 1918, pp. 25-93.

Bates, Henry and Robert I. Busenbark, *Parrots and Related Birds.* T.F.H. Publications, Neptune, New Jersey, 1978.

Beebe, M.B. and W. Beebe. *Our Search for a Wilderness.* Henry Holt and Co., London, 1910.

Belcher, Sir Charles and G.D. Smooker. "Birds of the Colony of Trinidad and Tobago." *The Ibis,* Vol. 78, 1936, pp. 1-35.

Berlepsch, Hans Graf von. "Beschreibung von zwei Neuen von den Herren Dr. Bluntschi und Peyer auf der Insel Marajo am Ausfluss des Amazonenstroms Gesammelten Vogelformen." *Ornithologische Monatsberichte,* Vol. 21, 1913, pp. 147-148.

Berlepsch, Hans Graf von and E. Hartert. "On the Birds of the Orinoco Region." *Novitates Zoologicae,* Vol. 9, 1902, pp. 1-135.

Bond, J. "Resident Birds of the Bay Islands of Spanish Honduras." *Proceedings of the Academy of Natural Science, Philadelphia,* Vol. 88, 1936, pp. 353-364.

Bull, John. "Exotic Birds in New York." *Wilson Bulletin,* Vol. 85, 1973, pp. 501-505.

Chapman, F.M. "Bird Life in Colombia." *Bulletin of the American Museum of Natural History,* Vol. XXXVI, 1917, pp. 1-730.

Chapman, Frank M. *Field Book of Birds of the Panama Canal Zone.* G.R. Putnam's Sons, New York, 1928.

Cherrie, G.K. "A Contribution to the Ornithology of the Orinoco Region." *Museum of the Brooklyn Institute of Arts and Science Bulletin,* Vol. 2, 1916, pp. 133-374.

Davis, L.I. *A Field Guide to the Birds of Mexico and Central America.* University of Texas Press, Austin, Texas 1972.

Dugand, A. "Aves del department del Atlantico, Colombia." *Caldasia,* Vol. 4 (26), 1947, pp. 499-648.

Dugand, A. and J. Borrero. "Aves de la Confluencia del Eagueta y Orteguaza (bas aerea de tres esquinas)." *Caldasia,* Vol. 5 (21), 1948, pp. 115-156.

Eisenman, E. and H. Loftin. "Birds of the Panama Canal Zone Area." *Florida Naturalist,* Vol. 41, 1968, pp. 57-60, 95.

Forshaw, Joseph, M. *Parrots of the World.* T.F.H. Publications, Neptune, New Jersey, 1977.

Franzius, Alexander von. "Ueber die Geographische Verbreitung der Vogel Costaricas und deren Lenensweise." *Journal fur Ornithologie,* Vol. 17, 1869, pp. 1-545.

French, Richard. *A Guide to the Birds of Trinidad and Tobago.* Livingston Publishers, Wynnewood, Pennsylvania, 1973.

Freud, Arthur. "Parrots and Other Hook-Bills." *American Cage-Bird Magazine,* October 1974, pp. 8.

Friedmann, H. and F.D. Smith. "A Contribution to the Ornithology of Northwestern Venezuela." *Proceedings of the U.S. National Museum,* Vol. 100, 1950, pp. 411-538.

Friedmann, H. and F.D. Smith. "A Further Contribution on the Ornithology of Northwestern Venezuela." *Proceedings of the U.S. National Museum,* Vol. 104, 1955, pp. 463-524.

Grant, P.R. "Late Breeding on the Tres Marias Islands." *Condor,* Vol. 68, 1966, pp. 249-257.

Grayson, A.J. "The Physical Geography and Natural History of the Islands of the Tres Marias." *Proceedings of the Boston Natural History Society,* Vol. 14, 1871, pp. 261-302.

Greene, Dr. W.T. *Parrots in Captivity.* 1884 (Reprint: T.F.H. Publications, Neptune, New Jersey, 1979.)

Hardy, John W. "California Exotic Birds." *Wilson Bulletin,* Vol. 85, 1973, pp. 506-512.

Hellmayr, C.E. "Birds of the Rio Madiera." *Novitates Zoologicae,* Vol. XVIII, 1910, pp. 257-428.

Hensel, Mickey. "Breeding the Double Yellow Heads." *American Cage-Bird Magazine,* October 1977, pp. 24-25.

Herklots, G.A.C. *The Birds of Trinidad and Tobago.* Collins, London, 1961.

The Yellow Naped Amazon, *A. o. auropalliata* (opposite), and the Panama Amazon, *A. o. panamensis* (above), are sometimes confused. *Auropalliata* and *parvipes* are the only two subspecies which have yellow in the nape area—a patch of color totally isolated from forehead and crown coloring. The Panama's nape is always green. Moreover, while both adult Panamas and Yellow Napes have yellow in the forehead region, the Yellow Nape has a bolder and more distinctly bright yellow.

151

Hettiger, John. "The Most Unforgettable Parrots in My Life." *American Cage-Bird Magazine*, August 1973, pp. 11-12.

Howell, T.R. "An Ecological Study of the Birds of the Lowland Pine Savanna and Adjacent Rain Forest in Northeastern Nicaragua." *Living Bird*, 10th Annual, 1972, pp. 185-242.

Ibering, H. von. "Catalogos da Fauna Braziliera." *Museu Paulista, S. Paula*, 1907, pp. 1-485.

Los Angeles Times, Classified Advertisements. Part V, March 9, 1979, p. 16.

Lowery, H. George, Jr. and Walter W. Dalquest. "Birds from the State of Veracruz, Mexico." *University of Kansas Publication of the Museum of Natural History*, Vol. 3, 1951, pp. 531-649.

McLoughlin, E. "Field Notes on the Breeding and Diet of some South American Parrots." *Foreign Birds*, Vol. 36, 1970, pp. 169-171 and 210-213.

Meyer de Schauensee, R. *Birds of Colombia*, Livingston Publishing Company, Wynnewood, Pennsylvania, 1964.

Miller, A.H. "The Tropical Avifauna of the Upper Magdelena Valley, Colombia." *Auk*, Vol. 64, 1947, pp. 351-381.

Monroe, Burt L. Jr. "A Distributional Survey of the Birds of Honduras." *Ornithological Monographs, No. 7*, American Ornithologists Union, 1968.

Monroe, B.L. and T.R. Howell. "Geographic Varieties in Middle American Parrots of the *Amazona ochrocephala* Complex." *Occasional Zoological Papers of the Louisiana State University*, No. 34, 1966, pp. 1-18.

Mulawka, Edward J. *Taming and Training Parrots*. T.F.H. Publications, Neptune, New Jersey, 1981.

Naumberg, Elsie M. "The Birds of Matto Grosso, Brazil." *Bulletin of the American Museum of Natural History*, Vol. 60, 1930, pp. 1-432.

Nelson, E.W. "Birds of the Tres Marias Islands." *North American Fauna No. 4*. U.S. Department of Agriculture Division of Biological Survey, No. 14, 1899, pp. 21-62.

Nelson, E.W. "Descriptions of Thirty New North American Birds in the Biological Survey Collection. *Auk*, Vol. 17, 1900, pp. 253-270.

Patrick, Leon. Letter to the Editor. *Aviculture*, Vol. 6-7, 1936-37, p. 73.

Peters, J.L. "An Ornithological Survey in the Carribean Lowlands of Honduras." *Bulletin of the Museum of Comparative Zoology,* Vol. 39, 1929, pp. 379-478.

Peters, J.L. *Birds of the World,* V. 3, Harvard University Press, Cambridge, 1937.

Pinto, O.M. de "Cadernos De Amazonia, 8, Estudo Critico e Catalogo Remissivo das Aves do Territorio Federal de Roraima." *Instituo Nacional de Pesquisas da Amazonia,* Manaus, Brazil, 1966.

Plath, Karl, and Malcolm Davis. *This is the Parrot.* T.F.H. Publications, Neptune, New Jersey, 1971.

Ridgeway, Robert. "The Birds of North and Middle America." *Bulletin of the U.S. National Museum,* Vol. VII, No. 5, 1916, pp. 1-541.

Ridgeway, Robert. "A Catalogue of a Collection of Birds made by Mr. Charles H. Townsend on Islands in the Caribbean and Honduras." *Proceedings of the U.S. National Museum,* Vol. 10, 1887, pp. 572-597.

Russel, Stephen M. "A Distributional Study of the Birds of British Honduras." *Ornithological Monograph No. 1,* The American Ornithologists' Union, 1964.

Salvin, O. "A List of the Birds of the Islands of the Coast of Yucatan and of the Bay of Honduras." *The Ibis,* 1889, pp. 359-379; 1890, pp. 84-95.

Salvin, O. "On the Ornithology of Guatemala." *The Ibis,* 1866, p. 195.

Salvin, O. "On the Psittacidae of Central America." *The Ibis,* Vol. 13, 1871, pp. 86-100.

Schafer, E. and W.H. Phelps. "Las Aves del Parque Nacional 'Henri Pittier' (Rancho Grande) y sus Funciones Ecologicas." *Bol. Soc. Venez. Cienc. Nat.,* Vol. 16, (83) pp. 3-167.

Schonwetter, M. *Handbuch der Zoologie.* Academie-Verlag. bd. 1, Lief 9, Berlin, 1964.

Sclater, P.L. and O. Salvin. "On the Ornithology of Central America." *The Ibis,* Vol. II, 1859, p. 138.

Slud, Paul. "The Birds of Costa Rica." *Bulletin of the American Museum of Natural History,* Vol. 128, 1964, pp. 1-430.

Smith, Clifford. "Breeding the Yellow Fronted Amazon." *Avicultural Magazine,* Vol. 73, 1967, pp. 199-200.

Limited solely to Las Tres Marias Islands off the western coast of Mexico, the Tres Marias Amazon, *A. o. tresmariae* (above), has an extremely small range; it is geographically isolated from other *ochrocephala* subspecies by several hundred kilometers. Since the extent of yellow is variable, depending on the maturity of the individual, the Tres Marias is often confused with the Double Yellow Head, *A. o. oratrix* (opposite), and with good reason. Aside from the brightness and tone of coloration of the head and upper breast regions, there is little other difference between the two races. As a matter of fact, the differences in color shade are so slight that experts are frequently confused.

Snyder, Dorothy E. *The Birds of Guyana*. Peabody Museum, Salem, 1966.

Stager, K.E. "The Avifauna of the Tres Marias Islands, Mexico." *Auk,* Vol. 74, 1957, pp. 413-432.

Stone, W. "The Birds of Honduras with Special Reference to a Collection made in 1930 by John Emlen and C. Brooke Worth." *Proceedings of the Academy of Natural Science, Philadelphia,* Vol. 84, 1932, pp. 291-342.

Sutton, G.M. *Mexican Birds.* University of Oklahoma Press, 1951.

Taylor, G.C. "On Birds Collected or Observed in the Republic of Honduras with a Short Account of a Journey Across the Country from the Pacific to the Atlantic Ocean." *The Ibis,* Vol. 8, 1860, pp. 10-24, 110-122, 222-228, 311-317.

Underwood, C.F. "A List of Birds Collected or Observed on the Lower, Southern and Southwestern Slopes of the Volcano of Miravalles and the Lower lands Extending to Bagaces in Costa Rica with a Few Observations on their Habits." *The Ibis,* Vol. 38, 1896, pp. 431-451.

Wetmore, Alexander. "The Birds of the Republic of Panama, Part II." *Smithsonian Miscellaneous Collections,* Vol. 150, 1968, pp. 1-605.

Wetmore, Alexander. "Observations of the Birds of Northern Venezuela." *Proceedings of the U.S. National Museum,* Vol. 87, 1939, pp. 173-260.

The raised head feathers are a characteristic expression of the Double Yellow Head, *A. o. oratrix.*